W9-AXZ-251

The Political Science Student Writer's Manual

Fifth Edition

Gregory M. Scott
Stephen M. Garrison
University of Central Oklahoma

PEARSON
Prentice
Hall

Upper Saddle River, New Jersey 07458

Library of Congress Cataloging-in-Publication Data

Scott, Gregory M.
   The political science student writer's manual / Gregory M. Scott, Stephen M.
Garrison.—5th ed.
     p. cm.
   Includes bibliographical references and index.
   ISBN 0-13-189259-2
   1. Political science—Authorship—Handbooks, manuals, etc. 2. Political science—Research—
Handbooks, manuals, etc. 3. Academic writing—Handbooks, manuals, etc. 4. Report writing—
Handbooks, manuals, etc. I. Garrison, Stephen M. II. Title.
   JA86.S39 2006
   808'.06632—dc22

                   2005014676

To Ariana and Luke

Editorial Director: Charlyce Jones Owens
Editorial Assistant: Suzanne Remore
Marketing Director: Heather Shelstedt
Marketing Assistant: Jennifer Lang
Senior Managing Editor: Lisa Iarkowski
Production Liaison: Fran Russello
Manufacturing Buyer: Sherry Lewis
Cover Design: Bruce Kenselaar
Cover Illustration/Photo: Getty Images, inc.
Composition/Full-Service Project Management: Shelley Creager/TechBooks

Credits and acknowledgments borrowed from other sources and reproduced, with permission, in this textbook appear on appropriate page within text.

This book was set in 10/12 Baskerville by TechBooks/York, PA Campus. It was printed and bound by Courier Companies Inc. The cover was printed by Courier Companies Inc.

10 9 8 7 6 5 4 3 2 1
ISBN 0-13-189259-2

Contents

To the Student

We have designed this book to help you do two things: (1) improve your writing, and (2) learn political science. Part One addresses fundamental concerns of all writers, exploring the reasons why we write, describing the writing process itself, and examining those elements of grammar, style, and punctuation that cause the most confusion among writers in general. A vital concern throughout this part, and the rest of the book as well, is the three-way interrelationship among writer, topic, and audience. Our discussion of this relationship aims at building your self-confidence as you clarify your writing objectives.

Writing is not a magical process beyond the control of most people. It is instead a series of interconnected skills that any writer can improve with practice, and the end result of this practice is power. Chapters 1 and 2 of this manual treat the act of writing not as an empty exercise undertaken only to produce a grade but as a powerful learning tool and the primary medium by which political scientists accomplish their goals. Chapter 3 explains the importance of formatting your writing properly and supplies you with format models for title pages, tables of contents, and so on. Chapter 4 explains how to cite sources and how to use source material ethically.

The chapters in Part Two of the book offer you general help in formulating and researching political science writing projects. Parts Three, Four, and Five structure writing assignments that will give you practice in using the materials provided in Part Two. We have based these assignments on the types of work political scientists actually do, both as academic professionals and as contributing citizens in local and in national political communities. The assignments will test your ability to think critically and come up with and express ideas that will improve all our lives.

Greg Scott
Steve Garrison

To the Teacher

This book helps you deal with three problems commonly faced by teachers of political science:

- Students increasingly need *specific direction* to produce a good paper.
- Political scientists, as always, want to *teach political science, not English*.
- Students do not yet understand fully how—and why—to avoid *plagiarism*.

Students often need substantial specific direction to produce a good paper. How many times have you assigned papers in your political science classes and found yourself teaching the basics of writing—not only in terms of content but form and grammar as well? This text, which may either accompany the primary text you assign in any class or stand on its own, allows you to assign one of the types of papers described in Parts Three, Four, and Five with the knowledge that virtually everything the student needs to know, from grammar to sources of information to reference style, is in this one volume.

Part One helps you to spend more time teaching political science and less time teaching English. It includes (1) a concise guide to writing well, (2) a summary of the most troublesome English grammar rules, (3) proper political science college paper formats, and (4) extensive instruction and examples on how to cite sources according to specifications published by the American Political Science Association (APSA).

Also, this book may well be your best insurance against plagiarism, for two reasons. First, Chapter 4, Section 2, provides a detailed, practical explanation of what plagiarism is and how to avoid it. Second, the paper assignments in Parts Three, Four, and Five of this manual provide very specific directions that make it much more difficult for students simply to appropriate uncredited material, even from the Internet, where, as you know, it is becoming easier for students to download relevant material and then modify it (insufficiently) for their own purposes.

In addition, this fifth edition is the ***most substantial revision*** of *The Political Science Student Writer's Manual* ever undertaken. Among the scores of changes throughout the volume, you will find the following:

- ***Updated citation specifications,*** including simplified instructions on how to cite Internet sources
- ***New information sources*** for writing, politics, government, and political science
- ***New, practical writing assignments*** for introductory students that help them participate in politics: *Letters to Editors, Op-ed Essays, and Letters to Representatives*
- ***New critical thinking exercises*** for introductory and advanced students, focusing on the philosophical tensions inherent in Plato's *Ring of Gyges*, Rawl's *veil of ignorance*, and Foucault's (Bentham's) *panopticon*
- A streamlining of inessential materials in order to reduce the price for cost-conscious students.

We hope you find that the fifth edition helps you in your efforts to teach political science. We wish you the best in your endeavors, and we welcome your comments.

Greg Scott
Steve Garrison

◆ CHAPTER 1 ◆

Writing as Communication

1.1   WRITING TO LEARN

Writing is a way of ordering your experience. Think about it. No matter what you are writing—it may be a paper for your American government class, a short story, a limerick, a grocery list—you are putting pieces of your world together in new ways and making yourself freshly conscious of those pieces. This is one of the reasons writing is so hard. From the infinite welter of data that your mind continually processes and locks in your memory, you are selecting only certain items significant to the task at hand, relating them to other items, and phrasing them with a new coherence. You are mapping a part of your universe that has hitherto been unknown territory. You are gaining a little more control over the processes by which you interact with the world around you.

This is why the act of writing, no matter what its result, is never insignificant. It is always *communication*—if not with another human being, then with yourself. It is a way of making a fresh connection with your world.

Writing therefore is also one of the best ways to learn. This statement may sound odd at first. If you are an unpracticed writer, you may share a common notion that the only purpose of writing is to express what you already know or think. According to this view, any learning that you as a writer might have experienced has already occurred by the time your pen meets the paper; your task is thus to inform and even surprise the reader. But, if you are a practiced writer, you know that at any moment as you write, you are capable of surprising yourself. And it is surprise that you look for: the shock of seeing what happens in your own mind when you drop an old, established opinion into a batch of new facts or bump into a cherished belief from a different angle. Writing synthesizes new understanding for the writer. E. M. Forster's famous question "How do I know what I think until I see what I say?" is one that all of us could ask. We make meaning as we write, jolting ourselves by little, surprising discoveries into a larger and more interesting universe.

The Irony of Writing

Good writing, especially good writing about politics, helps the reader become aware of the ironies and paradoxes of human existence. One such paradox is that good writing expresses both that which is unique about the writer and that which the writer shares with every human being. Many of our most famous political statements share this double attribute of mirroring the singular and the ordinary simultaneously. For example, read the following excerpt from President Franklin Roosevelt's first inaugural address, spoken on March 4, 1933, in the middle of the Great Depression, and then answer this question: Is Roosevelt's speech famous because its expression is extraordinary or because it appeals to something that is basic to every human being?

> This is pre-eminently the time to speak the truth, the whole truth, frankly and boldly. Nor need we shrink from honestly facing conditions in our country today. This great nation will endure as it has endured, will revive and will prosper.
>
> So first of all let me assert my firm belief that the only thing we have to fear is fear itself—nameless, unreasoning, unjustified terror which paralyzes needed efforts to convert retreat into advance.
>
> In every dark hour of our national life a leadership of frankness and vigor has met with that understanding and support of the people themselves which is essential to victory. I am convinced that you will again give that support to leadership in these critical days.
>
> In such a spirit on my part and on yours we face our common difficulties. They concern, thank God, only material things. Values have shrunken to fantastic levels; taxes have risen; our ability to pay has fallen; government of all kinds is faced by serious curtailment of income; the means of exchange are frozen in the currents of trade; the withered leaves of industrial enterprise lie on every side; farmers find no markets for their produce; the savings of many years in thousands of families are gone.
>
> More important, a host of unemployed citizens face the grim problem of existence, and an equally great number toil with little return. Only a foolish optimist can deny the dark realities of the moment.
>
> Yet our distress comes from no failure of substance. We are stricken by no plague of locusts. Compared with the perils which our forefathers conquered because they believed and were not afraid, we have still much to be thankful for. Nature still offers her bounty and human efforts have multiplied it. Plenty is at our doorstep, but a generous use of it languishes in the very sight of the supply. . . .
>
> The measure of the restoration lies in the extent to which we apply social values more noble than mere monetary profit.
>
> Happiness lies not in the mere possession of money; it lies in the joy of achievement, in the thrill of creative effort.
>
> The joy and moral stimulation of work no longer must be forgotten in the mad chase of evanescent profits. These dark days will be worth all they cost us if they teach us that our true destiny is not to be ministered unto but to minister to ourselves and to our fellow-men.(Roosevelt 1963, 240)

The help that writing gives us with learning and with controlling what we learn is one of the major reasons why your political science instructors will require a great deal of writing from you. Learning the complex and diverse world of the political scientist takes more than a passive ingestion of facts. You have to understand the processes of government, and come to grips with social issues and with your own attitudes toward them. When you write in a class on American government or public policy, you are entering into the world of political scientists in the same way they do—by testing theory against fact and fact against belief.

Writing is the means of entering political life. Virtually everything that happens in politics happens first on paper. Documents are wrestled into shape before their contents can affect the public. Great speeches are written before they are spoken. The written word has helped bring slaves to freedom, end wars, and shape the values of nations. Often, in politics as elsewhere, gaining recognition for ourselves and our ideas depends less on what we say than on how we say it. Accurate and persuasive writing is absolutely vital to the political scientist.

EXERCISE   **Learning by Writing**

One way of testing the notion that writing is a powerful learning tool is by rewriting your notes from a recent class lecture. The type of class does not matter; it can be history, chemistry, advertising, whatever. If possible, choose a difficult class, one in which you are feeling somewhat unsure of the material and for which you have taken copious notes.

As you rewrite, provide the transitional elements (connecting phrases such as *in order to, because of, and, but, however*) that you were unable to supply in class because of the press of time. Furnish your own examples or illustrations of the ideas expressed in the lecture.

This experiment will force you to supply necessary coherence to your own thought processes. See if the time it takes you to rewrite the notes is not more than compensated for by your increased understanding of the lecture material.

Challenge Yourself

There is no way around it: writing is a struggle. Did you think you were the only one to feel this way? Take heart! Writing is hard for everybody, great writers included. Bringing order to the world is never easy. Isaac Bashevis Singer, winner of the 1978 Nobel Prize in literature, once wrote: "I believe in miracles in every area of life except writing. Experience has shown me that there are no miracles in writing. The only thing that produces good writing is hard work" (quoted in Lunsford and Connors 1992, 2).

Hard work was evident in the words of John F. Kennedy's inaugural address. Each word was crafted to embed an image in the listener's mind. As you read the following excerpt from Kennedy's speech, what images does it evoke? Historians tend to consider a president "great" when his words live longer than his deeds in the minds of the people. Do you think this will be—or has been—true of Kennedy?

> We observe today not a victory of party but a celebration of freedom—
> symbolizing an end as well as a beginning—signifying renewal as well as

change. For I have sworn before you and Almighty God the same solemn oath our forebears prescribed nearly a century and three-quarters ago.

The world is very different now. For man holds in his mortal hands the power to abolish all forms of human poverty and all forms of human life. And yet the same revolutionary beliefs for which our forebears fought are still at issue around the globe—the belief that the rights of man come not from the generosity of the state but from the hand of God.

We dare not forget today that we are the heirs of that first revolution. Let the word go forth from this time and place, to friend and foe alike, that the torch has been passed to a new generation of Americans—born in this century, tempered by war, disciplined by a hard and bitter peace, proud of our ancient heritage—and unwilling to witness or permit the slow undoing of those human rights to which this nation has always been committed, and to which we are committed today at home and around the world. . . .

In the long history of the world, only a few generations have been granted the role of defending freedom in its hours of maximum danger. I do not shrink from this responsibility—I welcome it. I do not believe that any of us would exchange places with any other people or any other generation. The energy, the faith, the devotion which we bring to this endeavor will light our country and all who serve it—and the glow from that fire can truly light the world.

And so, my fellow Americans: ask not what your country can do for you—ask what you can do for your country.

My fellow citizens of the world: ask not what America will do for you, but what together we can do for the freedom of man. (Kennedy 1963, 688–89)

One reason that writing is difficult is that it is not actually a single activity at all but a process consisting of several activities that can overlap, with two or more sometimes operating simultaneously as you labor to organize and phrase your thoughts. (We will discuss these activities later in this chapter.) The writing process tends to be sloppy for everyone, an often-frustrating search for meaning and for the best way to articulate that meaning.

Frustrating though that search may sometimes be, it need not be futile. Remember this: the writing process uses skills that we all have. The ability to write, in other words, is not some magical competence bestowed on the rare, fortunate individual. Although few of us may achieve the proficiency of Isaac Bashevis Singer or John F. Kennedy, we are all capable of phrasing thoughts clearly and in a well-organized fashion. But learning how to do so takes practice.

The one sure way to improve your writing is to write.

One of the toughest but most important jobs in writing is to maintain enthusiasm for your writing project. Such commitment may sometimes be hard to achieve, given the difficulties that are inherent in the writing process and that can be made worse when the project is unappealing at first glance. How, for example, can you be enthusiastic about having to write a paper analyzing campaign financing for the 1998 congressional elections, when you have never once thought about campaign finances and can see no use in doing so now?

One of the worst mistakes that unpracticed student writers make is to fail to assume responsibility for keeping themselves interested in their writing. No matter how hard it may seem at first to drum up interest in your topic, you have to do it—

that is, if you want to write a paper you can be proud of, one that contributes useful material and a fresh point of view to the topic. One thing is guaranteed: if you are bored with your writing, your reader will be, too. So what can you do to keep your interest and energy level high?

Challenge yourself. Think of the paper not as an assignment but as a piece of writing that has a point to make. To get this point across persuasively is the real reason you are writing, not because a teacher has assigned you a project. If someone were to ask you why you are writing your paper and your immediate, unthinking response is, "Because I've been given a writing assignment" or "Because I want a good grade," or some other nonanswer along these lines, your paper may be in trouble.

If, on the other hand, your first impulse is to explain the challenge of your main point—"I'm writing to show how campaign finance reform will benefit every taxpayer in America"—then you are thinking usefully about your topic.

Maintain Self-Confidence

Having confidence in your ability to write well about your topic is essential for good writing. This does not mean that you will always know what the result of a particular writing activity will be. In fact, you have to cultivate your ability to tolerate a high degree of uncertainty while weighing evidence, testing hypotheses, and experimenting with organizational strategies and wording. Be ready for temporary confusion and for seeming dead ends, and remember that every writer faces these obstacles. It is out of your struggle to combine fact with fact, to buttress conjecture with evidence, that order will arise.

Do not be intimidated by the amount and quality of work that others have already done in your field of inquiry. The array of opinion and evidence that confronts you in the literature can be confusing. But remember that no important topic is ever exhausted. There are always gaps—questions that have not been satisfactorily explored in either the published research or the prevailing popular opinion. It is in these gaps that you establish your own authority, your own sense of control.

Remember that the various stages of the writing process reinforce each other. Establishing a solid motivation strengthens your sense of confidence about the project, which in turn influences how successfully you organize and write. If you start out well, use good work habits, and allow ample time for the various activities to coalesce, you should produce a paper that will reflect your best work, one that your audience will find both readable and useful.

1.2   THE WRITING PROCESS

The Nature of the Process

As you engage in the writing process, you are doing many things at once. While planning, you are no doubt defining the audience for your paper at the same time that you are thinking about its purpose. As you draft the paper, you may organize your next sentence while revising the one you have just written. Different parts of the writing process overlap, and much of the difficulty of writing occurs because so many things happen at once. Through practice—in other words, through *writing*—it is possible to learn how to control those parts of the process that can in fact be controlled and to encourage those mysterious, less controllable activities.

No two people go about writing in exactly the same way. It is important to recognize the routines—modes of thought as well as individual exercises—that help you negotiate the process successfully. It is also important to give yourself as much time as possible to complete the process. Procrastination is one of the writer's greatest enemies. It saps confidence, undermines energy, destroys concentration. Writing regularly and following a well-planned schedule as closely as possible often make the difference between a successful paper and an embarrassment.

Although the various parts of the writing process are interwoven, there is naturally a general order to the work of writing. You have to start somewhere! What follows is a description of the various stages of the writing process—planning, drafting, revising, editing, and proofreading—along with suggestions on how to approach each most successfully.

Planning

Planning includes all activities that lead to the writing of the first draft of a paper. The particular activities in this stage differ from person to person. Some writers, for instance, prefer to compile a formal outline before writing the draft. Others perform brief writing exercises to jump-start their imaginations. Some draw diagrams; some doodle. Later we will look at a few starting strategies, and you can determine which may help you.

Now, however, let us discuss certain early choices that all writers must make during the planning stage. These choices concern *topic, purpose, and audience,* elements that make up the writing context, or the terms under which we all write. Every time you write, even if you are only writing a diary entry or a note to the milkman, these elements are present. You may not give conscious consideration to all of them in each piece of writing that you do, but it is extremely important to think carefully about them when writing a political science paper. Some or all of these defining elements may be dictated by your assignment, yet you will always have a degree of control over them.

Selecting a Topic

No matter how restrictive an assignment may seem, there is no reason to feel trapped by it. Within any assigned subject you can find a range of topics to explore. What you are looking for is a topic that engages your own interest. Let your curiosity be your guide. If, for example, you have been assigned the subject of campaign finances, then guide yourself to find some issue concerning the topic that interests you. (For example, how influential are campaign finances in the average state senate race? What would be the repercussions of limiting financial contributions from special interest groups?) Any good topic comes with a set of questions; you may well find that your interest increases if you simply begin asking questions. One strong recommendation: ask your questions *on paper*. Like most mental activities, the process of exploring your way through a topic is transformed when you write down your thoughts as they come, instead of letting them fly through your mind unrecorded. Remember the words of Louis Agassiz: "A pen is often the best of eyes" (1958, 106).

Although it is vital to be interested in your topic, you do not have to know much about it at the outset of your investigation. In fact, having too heartfelt a commitment to a topic can be an impediment to writing about it; emotions can get in the way of objectivity. It is often better to choose a topic that has piqued your interest yet remained something of a mystery to you—a topic discussed in one of your classes, perhaps, or mentioned on television or in a conversation with friends.

Narrowing the Topic

The task of narrowing your topic offers you a tremendous opportunity to establish a measure of control over the writing project. It is up to you to hone your topic to just the right shape and size to suit both your own interests and the requirements of the assignment. Do a good job of it, and you will go a long way toward guaranteeing yourself sufficient motivation and confidence for the tasks ahead. However, if you do not do it well, somewhere along the way you may find yourself directionless and out of energy.

Generally, the first topics that come to your mind will be too large for you to handle in your research paper. For example, the subject of a national income security policy has recently generated a tremendous number of news reports. Yet despite all the attention, there is still plenty of room for you to investigate the topic on a level that has real meaning for you and that does not merely recapitulate the published research. What about an analysis of how one of the proposed income security policies might affect insurance costs in a locally owned company?

The problem with most topics is not that they are too narrow or have been too completely explored, but rather that they are so rich that it is often difficult to choose the most useful way to address them. Take some time to narrow your topic. Think through the possibilities that occur to you and, as always, jot down your thoughts.

Students in an undergraduate course on political theory were told to write an essay of 2,500 words on one of the following issues. Next to each general topic is an example of how students narrowed it into a manageable paper topic.

GENERAL TOPIC	NARROWED TOPIC
George W. Bush	Bush's view of the role of religion in politics
Freedom	A comparison of Jean Jacques Rousseau's concept of freedom with John Locke's
Interest Groups	The political power of the National Rifle Association
Bart Simpson	Bart Simpson's political ideology

EXERCISE   **Narrowing Topics**

Without doing research, see how you can narrow the following general topics:

EXAMPLE

General topic   The United Nations

Narrowed topics   The United Nations' intervention in civil wars

                       The United Nations' attempts to end starvation

                       The role of the United Nations in stopping nuclear proliferation

GENERAL TOPICS

War in Iraq	Gun control	Freedom of marriage
International terrorism	Political corruption	Abortion rights
Education	Military spending	
Freedom of speech	The budget deficit	

Finding a Thesis

As you plan your writing, be on the lookout for an idea that can serve as your thesis. A *thesis* is not a fact, which can be immediately verified by data, but an assertion worth discussing, an argument with more than one possible conclusion. Your thesis sentence will reveal to your reader not only the argument you have chosen, but also your orientation toward it and the conclusion that your paper will attempt to prove.

In looking for a thesis, you are doing many jobs at once:

1. You are limiting the amount and kind of material that you must cover, thus making them manageable.
2. You are increasing your own interest in the narrowing field of study.
3. You are working to establish your paper's purpose, the reason you are writing about your topic. (If the only reason you can see for writing is to earn a good grade, then you probably won't!)
4. You are establishing your notion of who your audience is and what sort of approach to the subject might best catch its interest.

In short, you are gaining control over your writing context. For this reason, it is a good idea to come up with a thesis early on, a *working thesis,* which will very probably change as your thinking deepens but which will allow you to establish a measure of order in the planning stage.

The Thesis Sentence.   The introduction of your paper will contain a sentence that expresses the task that you intend to accomplish. This *thesis sentence* communicates your main idea, the one you are going to prove, defend, or illustrate. It sets up an expectation in the reader's mind that it is your job to satisfy.

But, in the planning stage, a thesis sentence is more than just the statement that informs your reader of your goal: it is a valuable tool to help you narrow your focus and confirm in your own mind your paper's purpose.

Developing a Thesis

Students in a class on public policy analysis were assigned a twenty-page paper on a problem currently being faced by the municipal authorities in their own city. The choice of the problem was left to the students. One, Richard Cory, decided to investigate the problem posed by the large number of abandoned buildings in a downtown neighborhood through which he drove on his way to the university. His first working thesis was as follows:

Abandoned houses result in negative social effects to the city.

The problem with this thesis, as Richard found out, was that it was not an idea that could be argued, but rather a fact that could be easily corroborated by the sources he began to consult. As he read reports from such groups as the Urban Land Institute and the City Planning Commission, and talked with representatives from the Community Planning Department, he began to get interested in the dilemma his city faced in responding to the problem of abandoned buildings. Richard's second working thesis was as follows:

Removal of abandoned buildings is a major problem facing the city.

While his second thesis narrowed the topic somewhat and gave Richard an opportunity to use material from his research, there was still no real comment attached to it. It still stated a bare fact, easily proved. At this point, Richard became interested in the even narrower topic of how building removal should best be handled. He found that the major issue was funding and that different civic groups favored different methods of accomplishing this. As Richard explored the arguments for and against the various funding plans, he began to feel that one of them might be best for the city. As a result, Richard developed his third working thesis:

Assessing a demolition fee on each property offers a viable solution to the city's building removal problem.

Note how this thesis narrows the focus of Richard's paper even further than the other two had, while also presenting an arguable hypothesis. It tells Richard what he has to do in his paper, just as it tells his readers what to expect.

At some time during your preliminary thinking on a topic, you should consult the library to see how much published work on your issue exists. This search has at least two benefits:

1. It acquaints you with a body of writing that will become very important in the research phase of your paper.
2. It gives you a sense of how your topic is generally addressed by the community of scholars you are joining. Is the topic as important as you think it is? Has there been so much research on the subject as to make your inquiry, in its present formulation, irrelevant?

As you go about determining your topic, remember that one goal of your political science writing in college is always to enhance your own understanding of the political process, to build an accurate model of the way politics works. Let this goal help you to direct your research into those areas that you know are important to your knowledge of the discipline.

Defining a Purpose

There are many ways to classify the purposes of writing, but in general most writing is undertaken either to inform or to persuade an audience. The goal of informative, or expository, writing is simply to impart information about a particular subject, whereas the aim of persuasive writing is to convince your reader of your point of view on an issue. The distinction between expository and persuasive writing is not hard and fast, and most writing in political science has elements of both types. Most effective writing, however, is clearly focused on either exposition or persuasion. Position papers (arguments for adopting particular policies) for example, are designed to persuade, whereas policy analysis papers (Chapter 12) are meant to inform. When you begin writing, consciously select a primary approach of exposition or persuasion, and then set out to achieve that goal.

EXERCISE   **To Explain or to Persuade**

Can you tell from the titles of these two papers, both on the same topic, which is an expository paper and which is a persuasive paper?

1. Social Services Funding in the Second George W. Bush Administration
2. How the Second George W. Bush Administration Shifted Shares of Wealth in America

---

Again taking up the subject of campaign finances, let us assume that you must write a paper explaining how finances were managed in the 2004 Republican presidential campaign. If you are writing an expository paper, your task could be to describe as coherently and impartially as possible the methods by which the Republicans administered their campaign funds. If, however, you are attempting to convince your readers that the 2004 Republican campaign finances were criminally mismanaged by an elected official, you are writing to persuade, and your strategy will be radically different. Persuasive writing seeks to influence the opinions of its audience toward its subject.

Learn what you want to say. By the time you write your final draft, you must have a very sound notion of the point you wish to argue. If, as you write that final draft, someone were to ask you to state your thesis, you should be able to give a satisfactory answer with a minimum of delay and no prompting. If, on the other hand, you have to hedge your answer because you cannot easily express your thesis, you may not yet be ready to write a final draft. You may have to write a draft or two or engage in various prewriting activities to form a secure understanding of your task.

EXERCISE   Knowing What You Want to Say

Two writers have been asked to state the thesis of their papers. Which one better understands the writing task?

Writer 1:   "My paper is about tax reform for the middle class."
Writer 2:   "My paper argues that tax reform for the middle class would be unfair to the upper and lower classes, who would then have to share more responsibility for the cost of government."

Watch out for bias! There is no such thing as pure objectivity. You are not a machine. No matter how hard you may try to produce an objective paper, the fact is that every choice you make as you write is influenced to some extent by your personal beliefs and opinions. What you tell your readers is truth. In other words, it is influenced, sometimes without your knowledge, by a multitude of factors: your environment, upbringing, and education; your attitude toward your audience; your political affiliation; your race and gender; your career goals; and your ambitions for the paper you are writing. The influence of such factors can be very subtle, and it is something you must work to identify in your own writing as well as in the writing of others in order not to mislead or to be misled. Remember that one of the reasons for writing is *self-discovery*. The writing you will do in political science classes— as well as the writing you will do for the rest of your life—will give you a chance to discover and confront honestly your own views on your subjects. Responsible writers keep an eye on their own biases and are honest about them with their readers.

Defining Your Audience

In any class that requires you to write, you may sometimes find it difficult to remember that the point of your writing is not simply to jump through the technical hoops imposed by the assignment. The point is *communication*—the transmission of your knowledge and your conclusions to readers in a way that suits you. Your task is to pass on to your readers the spark of your own enthusiasm for your topic. Readers who were indifferent to your topic before reading your paper should look at it in a new way after finishing it. This is the great challenge of writing: to enter into a reader's mind and leave behind both new knowledge and new questions.

It is tempting to think that most writing problems would be solved if the writer could view the writing as if another person had produced it. The discrepancy between the understanding of the writer and that of the audience is the single greatest impediment to accurate communication. To overcome this barrier you must consider your audience's needs. By the time you begin drafting, most if not all of your ideas will have begun to attain coherent shape in your mind, so that virtually any words with which you try to express those ideas will reflect your thought accurately—to you. Your readers, however, do not already hold the conclusions that you have so painstakingly achieved. If you omit from your writing the material that is necessary to complete your readers' understanding of your argument, they may well be unable to supply that information themselves.

The potential for misunderstanding is present for any audience, whether it is made up of general readers, experts in the field, or your professor, who is reading in part to see how well you have mastered the constraints that govern the relationship between writer and reader. Make your presentation as complete as possible, bearing in mind your audience's knowledge of your topic.

Invention Strategies

We have discussed various methods of selecting and narrowing the topic of a paper. As your focus on a specific topic sharpens, you will naturally begin to think about the kinds of information that will go into the paper. In the case of papers that do not require formal research, this material will come largely from your own recollections. Indeed, one of the reasons instructors assign such papers is to convince you of the incredible richness of your memory, the vastness and variety of the "database" that you have accumulated and that, moment by moment, you continue to build.

So vast is your hoard of information that it can sometimes be difficult to find within it the material that would best suit your paper. In other words, finding out what you already know about a topic is not always easy. *Invention,* a term borrowed from classical rhetoric, refers to the task of discovering, or recovering from memory, such information. As we write, we go through some sort of invention procedure that helps us explore our topic. Some writers seem to have little problem coming up with material; others need more help. Over the centuries, writers have devised different exercises that can help locate useful material housed in memory. We will look at a few of these briefly.

Freewriting

Freewriting is an activity that forces you to get something down on paper. There is no waiting around for inspiration. Instead, you set a time limit—perhaps three to five minutes—and write for that length of time without stopping, not even to lift the pen from the paper or your hands from the keyboard. Focus on the topic, and do not let the difficulty of finding relevant material stop you from writing. If necessary, you may begin by writing, over and over, some seemingly useless phrase, such as, "I cannot think of anything to write," or perhaps the name of your topic. Eventually, something else will occur to you. (It is surprising how long a three-minute period of freewriting can seem to last!) At the end of the freewriting, look over what you have produced for anything you might be able to use. Much of the writing will be unusable, but there might be an insight or two that you did not know you had.

In addition to its ability to help you recover from your memory usable material for your paper, freewriting has certain other benefits. First, it takes little time, which means that you may repeat the exercise as often as you like. Second, it breaks down some of the resistance that stands between you and the act of writing. There is no initial struggle to find something to say; you just write.

Freewriting

For his second-year American government class, John Alexander had to write a paper on some aspect of local government. John, who felt his understanding of local government was slight, began the job of finding a topic that interested him with two minutes of freewriting. Thinking about local government, John wrote steadily for this period without lifting his pen from the paper. Here is the result of his freewriting:

Okay okay local government. Local, what does that mean? Like police? Chamber of Commerce? the mayor—whoever that is? judges? I got that parking ticket last year, went to court, had to pay it anyway, bummer. Maybe trace what happens to a single parking ticket—and my money. Find out the public officials who deal with it, from the traffic cop who gives it out to wherever it ends up. Point would be, what? Point point point. To find out how much the local government spends to give out and process a $35 parking ticket— how much do they really make after expenses, and where does that money go? Have to include cop's salary? judge's? Printing costs for ticket? Salary for clerk or whoever deals only with ticket. Is there somebody who lives whole life only processing traffic tickets? Are traffic tickets and parking tickets handled differently? Assuming the guy fights it. Maybe find out the difference in revenue between a contested and an uncontested ticket? Lots of phone calls to make. Who? Where to start?

Brainstorming

Brainstorming is simply the process of making a list of ideas about a topic. It can be done quickly and at first without any need to order items in a coherent pattern. The point is to write down everything that occurs to you as quickly and briefly as possible, using individual words or short phrases. Once you have a good-sized list of items, you can then group them according to relationships that you see among them. Brainstorming thus allows you to uncover both ideas stored in your memory and useful associations among those ideas.

Brainstorming

A professor in an international politics class asked his students to write a 700-word paper, in the form of a letter to be translated and published in a Warsaw newspaper, giving Polish readers useful advice about living in a democracy. One student, Melissa Jessup, started thinking about the assignment by brainstorming. First, she simply wrote down anything about life in a democracy that occurred to her:

voting rights	welfare	freedom of press
protest movements	everybody equal	minorities
racial prejudice	American Dream	injustice
the individual	no job security	lobbyists and PACs
justice takes time	psychological factors	aristocracy of wealth
size of bureaucracy		

Thinking through her list, Melissa decided to divide it into two separate lists: one devoted to positive aspects of life in a democracy; the other, to negative aspects. At this point she decided to discard some items that were redundant or did not seem to have much potential. As you can see, Melissa had some questions about where some of her items would fit:

POSITIVE	NEGATIVE
voting rights	aristocracy of wealth
freedom of the press	justice takes time
everybody equal	racial prejudice
American Dream	welfare
psychological factors	lobbyists and PACs
protest movements (positive?)	size of bureaucracy

At this point, Melissa decided that her topic would be about the ways in which money and special interests affect a democratically elected government. Which items on her lists would be relevant to her paper?

Asking Questions

It is always possible to ask most or all of the following questions about any topic: *Who? What? When? Where? Why? How?* They force you to approach the topic as a journalist does, setting it within different perspectives that can then be compared.

Asking Questions

A professor asked her class on the judicial process to write a paper describing the impact of Supreme Court clerks on the decision-making process. One student developed the following questions as he began to think about a thesis:

Who are the Supreme Court's clerks? (How old? What is their racial and gender mix? What are their politics?)

What are their qualifications for the job?

What exactly is their job?

When during the court term are they most influential?

Where do they come from? (Is there any geographical or religious pattern in the way they are chosen? Do certain law schools contribute a significantly greater number of clerks than others?)

How are they chosen? (Are they appointed? elected?)

When in their careers do they serve?

Why are they chosen as they are?

Who have been some influential court clerks? (Have any gone on to sit on the bench themselves?)

Can you think of other questions that would make for useful inquiry?

Maintaining Flexibility

As you engage in invention strategies, you are also performing other writing tasks. You are still narrowing your topic, for example, as well as making decisions that will affect your choice of tone or audience. You are moving forward on all fronts with each decision you make affecting the others. This means that you must be flexible enough to allow for slight adjustments in your understanding of the paper's development and of your goal. Never be so determined to prove a particular theory that you fail to notice when your own understanding of it changes. Stay objective.

Organizing Your Writing

A paper that contains all the necessary facts but presents them in an ineffective order will confuse rather than inform or persuade. Although there are various methods of grouping ideas, none is potentially more effective than outlining. Unfortunately, no organizing process is more often misunderstood.

Outlining for Yourself

Outlining can do two jobs. First, it can force you, the writer, to gain a better understanding of your ideas by arranging them according to their interrelationships. There is one primary rule of outlining: ideas of equal weight are placed on the same level within the outline. This rule requires you to determine the relative importance of your ideas. You have to decide which ideas are of the same type or order, and into which subtopic each idea best fits.

If, in the planning stage, you carefully arrange your ideas in a coherent outline, your grasp of your topic will be greatly enhanced. You will have linked your ideas logically together and given a basic structure to the body of the paper. This sort of subordinating and coordinating activity is difficult, however, and as a result, inexperienced writers sometimes begin to write their first draft without an effective outline, hoping for the best. This hope is usually unfulfilled, especially in complex papers involving research.

| EXERCISE | **Organizing Thoughts** |

Rodrigo, a student in a second-year class in government management, researched the impact of a worker-retraining program in his state and came up with the following facts and theories. Number them in logical order:

___ A growing number of workers in the state do not possess the basic skills and education demanded by employers.

___ The number of dislocated workers in the state increased from 21,000 in 1997 to 32,000 in 2006.

___ A public policy to retrain uneducated workers would allow them to move into new and expanding sectors of the state economy.

___ Investment in high technology would allow the state's employers to remain competitive in the production of goods and services in both domestic and foreign markets.

___ The state's economy is becoming more global and more competitive.

Outlining for Your Reader

The second job an outline can perform is to serve as a reader's blueprint to the paper, summarizing its points and their interrelationships. By consulting your outline, a busy policy maker can quickly get a sense of your paper's goal and the argument you have used to promote it. The clarity and coherence of the outline help determine how much attention your audience will give to your ideas.

As political science students, you will be given a great deal of help with the arrangement of your material into an outline to accompany your paper. A look at the formats presented in Chapter 3 of this manual will show you how strictly these formal outlines are structured. But, although you must pay close attention to these requirements, do not forget how powerful a tool an outline can be in the early planning stages of your paper.

The Formal Outline Pattern

Following this pattern accurately during the planning stage of your paper helps to guarantee that your ideas are placed logically:

Thesis sentence (precedes the formal outline)

  I. First main idea
    A. First subordinate idea
      1. Reason, example, or illustration
        a. Supporting detail
        b. Supporting detail
        c. Supporting detail
      2. Reason, example, or illustration
        a. Supporting detail
        b. Supporting detail
        c. Supporting detail
    B. Second subordinate idea
 II. Second main idea

Notice that each level of the paper must have more than one entry; for every A there must be at least a B (and, if required, a C, a D, and so on), and for every 1 there must be a 2. This arrangement forces you to *compare ideas,* looking carefully at each one to determine its place among the others. The insistence on assigning relative values to your ideas is what makes an outline an effective organizing tool.

The Patterns of Political Science Papers

The structure of any particular type of political science paper is governed by a formal pattern. When rigid external controls are placed on their writing, some writers feel that their creativity is hampered by a kind of "paint-by-numbers" approach to structure. It is vital to the success of your paper that you never allow yourself to be overwhelmed by the pattern rules for any type of paper. Remember that such controls exist not to limit your creativity but to make the paper immediately and easily useful to its intended audience. It is as necessary to write clearly and confidently in a position paper or a policy analysis paper as in a term paper for English literature, a résumé, a short story, or a job application letter.

Drafting

The Rough Draft

The planning stage of the writing process is followed by the writing of the first draft. Using your thesis and outline as direction markers, you must now weave your amalgam of ideas, data, and persuasion strategies into logically ordered sentences and paragraphs. Although adequate prewriting may facilitate drafting, it still will not be easy. Writers establish their own individual methods of encouraging themselves to forge ahead with the draft, but here are some tips:

1. *Remember that this is a rough draft, not the final paper.* At this stage, it is not necessary that every word be the best possible choice. Do not put that sort of pressure on yourself. You must not allow anything to slow you down now. Writing is not like sculpting in stone, where every chip is permanent; you can always go back to your draft and add, delete, reword, and rearrange. *No matter how much effort you have put into planning, you cannot be sure how much of this first draft you will eventually keep.* It may take several drafts to get one that you find satisfactory.

2. *Give yourself sufficient time to write.* Do not delay the first draft by telling yourself there is still more research to do. You cannot uncover all the material there is to know on a particular subject, so do not fool yourself into trying. Remember that writing is a process of discovery. You may have to begin writing before you can see exactly what sort of research you need to do. Keep in mind that there are other tasks waiting for you after the first draft is finished, so allow for them as you determine your writing schedule.

It is also very important to give yourself time to write, because the more time that passes after you have written a draft, the better your ability to view it with objectivity. It is very difficult to evaluate your writing accurately soon after you complete it. You need to cool down, to recover from the effort of putting all those words together. The "colder" you get on your writing, the better you are able to read it as if it were written by someone else and thus acknowledge the changes you will need to make to strengthen the paper.

3. *Stay sharp.* Keep in mind the plan you created as you narrowed your topic, composed a thesis sentence, and outlined the material. But, if you begin to feel a strong need to change the plan a bit, do not be afraid to do so. Be ready for surprises dealt you by your own growing understanding of your topic. Your goal is to record your best thinking on the subject as accurately as possible.

Language Choices

To be convincing, your writing has to be authoritative; that is, you have to sound as if you have complete confidence in your ability to convey your ideas in words. Sentences that sound stilted, or that suffer from weak phrasing or the use of clichés, are not going to win supporters for the positions that you express in your paper. So a major question becomes, How can I sound confident?

Here are some points to consider as you work to convey to your reader that necessary sense of authority:

Level of Formality.   Tone is one of the primary methods by which you signal to the readers who you are and what your attitude is toward them and toward your topic. Your major decision is which level of language formality is most appropriate to your audience. The informal tone you would use in a letter to a friend might well be out of place in a paper on "Waste in Military Spending" written for your government professor. Remember that tone is only part of the overall decision that you make about how to present your information. Formality is, to some extent, a function of individual word choices and phrasing. For example, is it appropriate to use contractions such as *isn't* or *they'll?* Would the strategic use of a sentence fragment for effect be out of place? The use of informal language, the personal *I,* and the second-person *you* is traditionally forbidden—for better or worse—in certain kinds of writing. Often, part of the challenge of writing a formal paper is simply how to give your prose impact while staying within the conventions.

Jargon.   One way to lose readers quickly is to overwhelm them with *jargon*—phrases that have a special, usually technical meaning within your discipline but that are unfamiliar to the average reader. The very occasional use of jargon may add an effective touch of atmosphere, but anything more than that will severely dampen a reader's enthusiasm for the paper. Often the writer uses jargon in an effort to impress the reader by sounding lofty or knowledgeable. Unfortunately, all jargon usually does is cause confusion. In fact, the use of jargon indicates a writer's lack of connection to the audience.

Political science writing is a haven for jargon. Perhaps writers of policy analyses and position papers believe their readers are all completely attuned to their terminology. Or some may hope to obscure damaging information or potentially unpopular ideas in confusing language. In other cases the problem could simply be unclear thinking by the writer. Whatever the reason, the fact is that political science papers too often sound like prose made by machines to be read by machines.

Students may feel that, to be accepted as political scientists, their papers should conform to the practices of their published peers. *This is a mistake.* Remember that it is never better to write a cluttered or confusing sentence than a clear one, and burying your ideas in jargon defeats the effort that you went through to form them.

EXERCISE   **Revising Jargon**

What words in the following sentence, from an article in a political science journal, are jargon? Can you rewrite it to clarify its meaning?

> The implementation of statute-mandated regulated inputs exceeds the conceptualization of the administrative technicians.

Clichés.   In the heat of composition, as you are looking for words to help you form your ideas, it is sometimes easy to plug in a *cliché*—a phrase that has attained universal recognition by overuse. (*Note:* Clichés differ from jargon in that clichés are part of the general public's everyday language, whereas jargon is specific to the language of experts in a field.) Our vocabularies are brimming with clichés:

It's *raining cats and dogs.*
That issue is as *dead as a doornail.*
It's time for the governor to *face the music.*
Angry voters *made a beeline* for the ballot box.

The problem with clichés is that they are virtually meaningless. Once colorful means of expression, they have lost their color through overuse, and they tend to bleed energy and color from the surrounding words. When revising, replace clichés with fresh wording that more accurately conveys your point.

Descriptive Language. Language that appeals to readers' senses will always engage their interest more fully than language that is abstract. This is especially important for writing in disciplines that tend to deal in abstracts, such as political science. The typical political science paper, with its discussions of principles, demographics, or points of law, is usually in danger of floating off into abstraction, with each paragraph drifting further away from the felt life of the readers. Whenever appropriate, appeal to your readers' sense of sight, hearing, taste, touch, or smell.

EXERCISE   **Using Descriptive Language**

Which of these two sentences is more effective?

1. The housing project had deteriorated badly since the last inspection.
2. The housing project had deteriorated badly since the last inspection; stench rose from the plumbing, grime coated the walls and floors, and rats scurried through the hallways.

Sexist Language. Language can be a very powerful method of either reinforcing or destroying cultural stereotypes. By treating the sexes in subtly different ways in your language, you may unknowingly be committing an act of discrimination. A common example is the use of the pronoun *he* to refer to a person whose gender has not been identified.

Some writers, faced with this dilemma, alternate the use of male and female personal pronouns; others use the plural to avoid the need to use a pronoun of either gender:

SEXIST	**NONSEXIST**
A lawyer should always treat his client with respect.	A lawyer should always treat his or her client with respect.
	Lawyers should always treat their clients with respect.
Man is a political animal.	People are political animals.

Remember that language is more than the mere vehicle of your thought. Your words shape perceptions for your readers. How well you say something will profoundly affect your readers' response to what you say. Sexist language denies to a large number of your readers the basic right to fair and equal treatment. Make sure your writing is not guilty of this form of discrimination.

Revising

Revising is one of the most important steps in ensuring the success of your essay. Although unpracticed writers often think of revision as little more than making sure all the *i*'s are dotted and *t*'s are crossed, it is much more than that. Revising is *reseeing* the essay, looking at it from other perspectives, trying always to align your view with the one that will be held by your audience. Research indicates that we are actually revising all the time, in every phase of the writing process, as we reread phrases, rethink the placement of an item in an outline, or test a new topic sentence for a paragraph. Subjecting your entire hard-fought draft to cold, objective scrutiny is one of the toughest activities to master, but it is absolutely necessary. You have to make sure that you have said everything that needs to be said clearly and logically. One confusing passage, and the reader's attention is deflected from where you want it to be. Suddenly the reader has to become a detective, trying to figure out why you wrote what you did and what you meant by it. You do not want to throw such obstacles in the path of understanding.

Here are some tips to help you with revision:

1. *Give yourself adequate time for revision.* As discussed above, you need time to become "cold" on your paper in order to analyze it objectively. After you have written your draft, spend some time away from it. Then try to reread it as if someone else had written it.

2. *Read the paper carefully.* This is tougher than it sounds. One good strategy is to read it aloud yourself or to have a friend read it aloud while you listen. (Note, however, that friends are usually not the best critics. They are rarely trained in revision techniques and are often unwilling to risk disappointing you by giving your paper a really thorough examination.)

3. *Have a list of specific items to check.* It is important to revise in an orderly fashion, in stages, first looking at large concerns, such as the overall organization, and then at smaller elements, such as paragraph or sentence structure.

4. *Check for unity*—the clear and logical relation of all parts of the essay to its thesis. Make sure that every paragraph relates well to the whole of the paper and is in the right place.

5. *Check for coherence.* Make sure there are no gaps between the various parts of the argument. Look to see that you have adequate transitions everywhere they are needed. Transitional elements are markers indicating places where the paper's focus or attitude changes. Such elements can take the form of one word—*however, although, unfortunately, luckily*—or an entire sentence or a paragraph: *In order to fully appreciate the importance of democracy as a shaping presence in post–Cold War Polish politics, it is necessary to examine briefly the Poles' last historical attempt to implement democratic government.*

Transitional elements rarely introduce new material. Instead, they are direction pointers, either indicating a shift to new subject matter or signaling how the writer wishes certain material to be interpreted by the reader. Because you, the writer, already know where and why your paper changes direction and how you want particular passages to be received, it can be very difficult for you to catch those places where transition is needed.

6. *Avoid unnecessary repetition.* Two types of repetition can annoy a reader: repetition of content and repetition of wording.

Repetition of content occurs when you return to a subject you have already discussed. Ideally, you should deal with a topic once, memorably, and then move on to your next subject. Organizing a paper is a difficult task, however, which usually occurs through a process of enlightenment in terms of purposes and strategies, and repetition of content can happen even if you have used prewriting strategies. What is worse, it can be difficult for you to be aware of the repetition in your own writing. As you write and revise, remember that any unnecessary repetition of content in your final draft is potentially annoying to your readers, who are working to make sense of the argument they are reading and do not want to be distracted by a passage repeating material they have already encountered. You must train yourself, through practice, to look for material that you have repeated unnecessarily.

Repetition of wording occurs when you overuse certain phrases or words. This can make your prose sound choppy and uninspired, as the following examples demonstrate:

> The subcommittee's report on education reform will surprise a number of people. A number of people will want copies of the report.

> The chairman said at a press conference that he is happy with the report. He will circulate it to the local news agencies in the morning. He will also make sure that the city council has copies.

> I became upset when I heard how the committee had voted. I called the chairman and expressed my reservations about the committee's decision. I told him I felt that he had let the teachers and students of the state down. I also issued a press statement.

The last passage illustrates a condition known by composition teachers as the *I-syndrome.* Can you hear how such duplicated phrasing can hurt a paper? Your language should sound fresh and energetic. Make sure, before you submit your final draft, to read through your paper carefully, looking for such repetition. However, not all repetition is bad. You may wish to repeat a phrase for rhetorical effect or special emphasis: "*I came. I saw. I conquered.*" Just make sure that any repetition in your paper is intentional, placed there to produce a specific effect.

Editing

Editing is sometimes confused with the more involved process of revising. But editing is done later in the writing process, after you have wrestled through your first draft—and maybe your second and third—and arrived at the final draft. Even though your draft now contains all the information you want to impart and has the information arranged to your satisfaction, there are still many factors to check, such as sentence structure, spelling, and punctuation.

It is at this point that an unpracticed writer might be less than vigilant. After all, most of the work on the paper is finished, as the "big jobs" of discovering, organizing, and drafting information have been completed. *But watch out!* Editing is as important as any other part of the writing process. Any error that you allow in the final draft will count against you in the mind of the reader. This may not seem fair, but even a minor error—a misspelling or confusing placement of a comma— will make a much greater impression on your reader than perhaps it should. Remember that everything about your paper is your responsibility, including performing even the supposedly little jobs correctly. Careless editing undermines the effectiveness of your paper. It would be a shame if all the hard work you put into prewriting, drafting, and revising were to be damaged because you carelessly allowed a comma splice!

Most of the tips given above for revising hold for editing as well. It is best to edit in stages, looking for only one or two kinds of errors each time you reread the paper. Focus especially on errors that you remember committing in the past. If, for instance, you know that you have a tendency to misplace commas, go through your paper looking at each comma carefully. If you have a weakness for writing unintentional sentence fragments, read each sentence aloud to make sure that it is indeed a complete sentence. Have you accidentally shifted verb tenses anywhere, moving from past to present tense for no reason? Do all the subjects in your sentences agree in number with their verbs? *Now is the time to find out.*

Watch out for *miscues*—problems with a sentence that the writer simply does not see. Remember that your search for errors is hampered in two ways:

1. As the writer, you hope not to find any errors in your work. This desire can cause you to miss mistakes when they do occur.
2. Because you know your material so well, it is easy, as you read, to unconsciously supply missing material—a word, a piece of punctuation—as if it were present.

How difficult is it to see that something is missing in the following sentence?

Unfortunately, legislators often have too little regard their constituents.

We can guess that the missing word is probably *for,* which should be inserted after *regard.* It is quite possible, however, that the writer of the sentence would automatically supply the missing *for* as if it were on the page. This is a miscue, which can be hard for writers to spot because they are so close to their material.

One tactic for catching mistakes in sentence structure is to read the sentences aloud, starting with the last one in the paper and then moving to the next-to-last, then to the previous sentence, and thus going backward through the paper (reading each sentence in the normal, left-to-right manner, of course) until you reach the first sentence of the introduction. This backward progression strips each sentence of its rhetorical context and helps you to focus on its internal structure.

Editing is the stage where you finally answer those minor questions that you had put off when you were wrestling with wording and organization. Any ambiguities regarding the use of abbreviations, italics, numerals, capital letters, titles (When do you capitalize the title *president*, for example?), hyphens, dashes (usually created on a typewriter or computer by striking the hyphen key twice), apostrophes, and quotation marks have to be cleared up now. You must also check to see that you have used the required formats for footnotes, endnotes, margins, page numbers, and the like.

Guessing is not allowed. Sometimes unpracticed writers who realize that they do not quite understand a particular rule of grammar, punctuation, or format do nothing to fill that knowledge gap. Instead they rely on guesswork and their own logic—which is not always up to the task of dealing with so contrary a language as English—to get them through problems that they could solve if they referred to a writing manual. Remember that it does not matter to the reader why or how an error shows up in your writing. It only matters that you have dropped your guard. You must not allow a careless error to undo all the good work that you have done.

Proofreading

Before you hand in the final version of your paper, it is vital that you check it one more time to make sure there are no errors of any sort. This job is called *proofreading*, or *proofing*. In essence, you are looking for many of the same things you had checked for during editing, but now you are doing it on the last draft, which is about to be submitted to your audience. Proofreading is as important as editing; you may have missed an error that you still have time to find, or an error may have been introduced when the draft was recopied or typed for the last time. Like every other stage of the writing process, proofreading is your responsibility.

At this point, you must check for typing mistakes: transposed or deleted letters, words, phrases, or punctuation. If you have had the paper professionally typed, you still must check it carefully. Do not rely solely on the typist's proofreading. If you are creating your paper on a computer or a word processor, it is possible for you to unintentionally insert a command that alters your document drastically by slicing out a word, line, or sentence at the touch of a key. Make sure such accidental deletions have not occurred.

Above all else, remember that your paper represents you. It is a product of your best thinking, your most energetic and imaginative response to a writing challenge. If you have maintained your enthusiasm for the project and worked through the stages of the writing process honestly and carefully, you should produce a paper you can be proud of, one that will serve its readers well.

◆ CHAPTER 2 ◆
Writing Competently

2.1   GRAMMAR AND STYLE

The Competent Writer

Good writing places your thoughts in your readers' minds in exactly the way you want them to be there. Good writing tells your readers just what you want them to know without telling them anything you do not want them to know. This may sound odd, but the fact is that writers have to be careful not to let unwanted messages slip into their writing. Look, for example, at the passage below, taken from a paper analyzing the impact of a worker-retraining program. Hidden within the prose is a message that jeopardizes the paper's success. Can you detect the message?

Recent articles written on the subject of dislocated workers have had little to say about the particular problems dealt with in this paper. Because few of these articles focus on the problem at the state level.

Chances are, when you reached the end of the second "sentence," you felt that something was missing and perceived a gap in logic or coherence, so you went back through both sentences to find the place where things had gone wrong. The second sentence is actually not a sentence at all. It does have certain features of a sentence—for example, a subject (*few*) and a verb (*focus*)—but its first word (*Because*) subordinates the entire clause that follows, taking away its ability to stand on its own as a complete idea. The second "sentence," which is properly called a *subordinate clause*, merely fills in some information about the first sentence, telling us why recent articles about dislocated workers fail to deal with problems discussed in the present paper.

The sort of error represented by the second "sentence" is commonly called a *sentence fragment,* and it conveys to the reader a message that no writer wants to send: that the writer either is careless or, worse, has not mastered the language. Language errors such as fragments, misplaced commas, or shifts in verb tense send out warnings in readers' minds. As a result, readers lose some of their concentration on the issue being discussed; they become distracted and begin to wonder about the language competency of the writer. The writing loses effectiveness.

NOTE. Whatever goal you set for your paper—be it to persuade, describe, analyze, or speculate—you must also set one other goal: *to display language competence.* If your paper does not meet this goal, it will not completely achieve its other aims. Language errors spread doubt like a virus; they jeopardize all the hard work you have done on your paper.

Language competence is especially important in political science, for credibility in politics depends on such skill. Anyone who doubts this should remember the beating that Vice President Dan Quayle took in the press for misspelling the word *potato* at a 1992 spelling bee. His error caused a storm of humiliating publicity for the hapless Quayle, adding to an impression of his general incompetence.

Correctness Is Relative

Although they may seem minor, the sort of language errors we are discussing—often called *surface errors*—can be extremely damaging in certain kinds of writing. Surface errors come in a variety of types, including misspellings, punctuation problems, grammar errors, and the inconsistent use of abbreviations, capitalization, and numerals. These errors are an affront to your readers' notion of correctness, and therein lies one of the biggest problems with surface errors. Different audiences tolerate different levels of correctness. You know that you can get away with surface errors in, say, a letter to a friend, who will probably not judge you harshly for them, whereas those same errors in a job application letter might eliminate you from consideration for the position. Correctness depends to an extent on context.

Another problem is that the rules governing correctness shift over time. What would have been an error to your grandmother's generation—the splitting of an infinitive, for example, or the ending of a sentence with a preposition—is taken in stride by most readers today.

So how do you write correctly when the rules shift from person to person and over time? Here are some tips:

Consider Your Audience

One of the great risks of writing is that even the simplest of choices regarding wording or punctuation can sometimes prejudice your audience against you in ways that may seem unfair. For example, look again at the old grammar rule forbidding the splitting of infinitives. After decades of telling students to never split an infinitive (something just done in this sentence), most composition experts now concede that a split infinitive is *not* a grammar crime. But suppose you have written a position paper trying to convince your city council of the need to hire security personnel for the library, and half of the council members—the people you wish to convince—remember their eighth-grade grammar teacher's warning about splitting infinitives. How will they respond when you tell them, in your introduction, that librarians are compelled *"to always accompany"* visitors to the rare book room because of the threat of vandalism? How much of their attention have you suddenly lost because of their automatic recollection of what is now a nonrule? It is possible, in other words, to write correctly and still offend your readers' notions of language competence.

Make sure that you tailor the surface features and the degree of formality of your writing to the level of competency that your readers require. When in doubt, take a conservative approach. Your audience might be just as distracted by a contraction as by a split infinitive.

Aim for Consistency

When dealing with a language question for which there are different answers—such as whether to use a comma before the conjunction in a series of three ("The mayor's speech addressed taxes, housing for the poor, and the job situation.")—always use the same strategy throughout your paper. If, for example, you avoid splitting one infinitive, avoid splitting *all* infinitives.

Have Confidence in What You Know about Writing!

It is easy for unpracticed writers to allow their occasional mistakes to shake their confidence in their writing ability. The fact is, however, that most of what we know about writing is correct. We are all capable, for example, of writing grammatically sound phrases, even if we cannot list the rules by which we achieve coherence. Most writers who worry about their chronic errors make fewer mistakes than they think. Becoming distressed about errors makes writing even more difficult.

Grammar

As various composition theorists have pointed out, the word *grammar* has several definitions. One meaning is "the formal patterns in which words must be arranged in order to convey meaning." We learn these patterns very early in life and use them spontaneously, without thinking. Our understanding of grammatical patterns is extremely sophisticated, despite the fact that few of us can actually cite the rules by which the patterns work. Patrick Hartwell tested grammar learning by asking native English speakers of different ages and levels of education, including high school teachers, to arrange these words in natural order:

French the young girls four

Everyone could produce the natural order for this phrase: "the four young French girls." Yet none of Hartwell's respondents said they knew the rule that governs the order of the words (Hartwell 1985, 111).

Eliminate Chronic Errors

But if just thinking about our errors has a negative effect on our writing, how do we learn to write more correctly? Perhaps the best answer is simply to write as often as possible. Give yourself lots of practice in putting your thoughts into written shape—and then in revising and proofing your work. As you write and revise, be honest with yourself—and patient. Chronic errors are like bad habits; getting rid of them takes time.

You probably know of one or two problem areas in your writing that you could have eliminated but have not. Instead, you may have "fudged" your writing at the critical points, relying on half-remembered formulas from past English classes or trying to come up with logical solutions to your writing problems. (*Warning:* The English language does not always work in a way that seems logical.) You may have simply decided that comma rules are unlearnable or that you will never understand the difference between the verbs *lay* and *lie.* And so you guess, and you come up with the wrong answer a good part of the time. What a shame, when just a little extra work would give you mastery over those few gaps in your understanding and boost your confidence as well.

Instead of continuing with this sort of guesswork and living with the holes in your knowledge, why not face the problem areas now and learn the rules that have heretofore escaped you? What follows is a discussion of those surface features of writing in which errors most commonly occur. You will probably be familiar with most if not all of the rules discussed, but there may well be a few you have not yet mastered. Now is the time to do so.

2.2   PUNCTUATION

Apostrophes

An apostrophe is used to show possession. When you wish to say that something belongs to someone or something, you add either an apostrophe and an *s* or an apostrophe alone to the word that represents the owner.

When the owner is singular (a single person or thing), the apostrophe precedes an added *s:*

> According to Mayor Anderson's secretary, the news broadcast has been canceled.

> The union's lawyers challenged the government's policy in court.
> Somebody's briefcase was left in the auditorium.

The same rule applies if the word showing possession is a plural that does not end in *s:*

> The women's club sponsored several debates during the last presidential campaign.

> Governor Smith has proven himself a tireless worker for children's rights.

When the word expressing ownership is a plural ending in *s,* the apostrophe follows the *s:*

The new legislation was discussed at the secretaries' conference.

There are two ways to form the possessive for two or more nouns:

1. To show joint possession (both nouns owning the same thing or things), the last noun in the series is possessive:

The president and first lady's invitations were sent out yesterday.

2. To indicate that each noun owns an item or items individually, each noun must show possession:

Mayor Scott's and Mayor MacKay's speeches took different approaches to the same problem.

The importance of the apostrophe is obvious when you consider the difference in meaning between the following two sentences:

Be sure to pick up the senator's bags on your way to the airport.
Be sure to pick up the senators' bags on your way to the airport.

In the first sentence, you have only one senator to worry about, whereas in the second, you have at least two!

A Prepostrophe?

James Swanson, political commentator and editor of the *Gesundheit Gazette,* occasionally encounters political statements that he finds to be preposterous. He believes that journalists should warn us when they print one of these statements by placing a "prepostrophe" (^) at the end of a preposterous sentence. Consider, for example, how a prepostrophe might assist the reader in the following statement: "We can cut taxes without reducing services^" For even more preposterous statements, we add more prepostrophes, as in, "I never had sex with that woman ^ ^"

Capitalization

Here is a brief summary of some hard-to-remember capitalization rules:

1. You may, if you choose, capitalize the first letter of the first word in a sentence that follows a colon. However, make sure you use one pattern consistently throughout your paper:

Our instructions are explicit: *Do not* allow anyone into the conference without an identification badge.

Our instructions are explicit: *do not* allow anyone into the conference without an identification badge.

2. Capitalize *proper nouns* (names of specific people, places, or things) and *proper adjectives* (adjectives made from proper nouns). A common noun following a proper adjective is usually not capitalized, nor is a common adjective preceding a proper adjective (such as *a, an,* or *the*):

PROPER NOUNS	PROPER ADJECTIVES
Poland	Polish officials
Iraq	the Iraqi ambassador
Shakespeare	a Shakespearean tragedy

Proper nouns include:

- *Names of monuments and buildings:* the Washington Monument, the Empire State Building, the Library of Congress
- *Historical events, eras, and certain terms concerning calendar dates:* the Civil War, the Dark Ages, Monday, December, Columbus Day
- *Parts of the country:* North, Southwest, Eastern Seaboard, the West Coast, New England

NOTE. When words like *north, south, east, west,* and *northwest* are used to designate direction rather than geographical region, they are not capitalized: "We drove east to Boston and then made a tour of the East Coast."

- *Words referring to race, religion, and nationality:* Islam, Muslim, Caucasian, White (or white), Asian, Negro, Black (or black), Slavic, Arab, Jewish, Hebrew, Buddhism, Buddhists, Southern Baptists, the Bible, the Koran, American
- *Names of languages:* English, Chinese, Latin, Sanskrit
- *Titles of corporations, institutions, universities, and organizations:* Dow Chemical, General Motors, the National Endowment for the Humanities, University of Tennessee, Colby College, Kiwanis Club, American Association of Retired Persons, Oklahoma State Senate

NOTE. Some words once considered proper nouns or adjectives have, over time, become common and are no longer capitalized, such as *french fries, pasteurized milk, arabic numerals,* and *italics.*

3. Titles of individuals may be capitalized if they precede a proper name; otherwise, titles are usually not capitalized:

The committee honored Senator Jones.

The committee honored the senator from Kansas.

We phoned Doctor Jessup, who arrived shortly afterward.

We phoned the doctor, who arrived shortly afterward.

A story on Queen Elizabeth's health appeared in yesterday's paper.

A story on the queen's health appeared in yesterday's paper.

Pope John Paul's visit to Colorado was a public relations success.

The pope's visit to Colorado was a public relations success.

When Not to Capitalize

In general, you do not capitalize nouns when your reference is nonspecific. For example, you would not capitalize *the senator,* but you would capitalize *Senator Smith.* The second reference is as much a title as it is a term of identification, whereas the first reference is a mere identifier. Likewise, there is a difference in degree of specificity between *the state treasury* and *the Texas State Treasury.*

NOTE. The meaning of a term may change somewhat depending on its capitalization. What, for example, might be the difference between a *Democrat* and a *democrat?* When capitalized, the word refers to a member of a specific political party; when not capitalized, it refers to someone who believes in the democratic form of government.

Capitalization depends to some extent on the context of your writing. For example, if you are writing a policy analysis for a specific corporation, you may capitalize words and phrases that refer to that corporation—such as *Board of Directors, Chairman of the Board,* and *the Institute*—that would not be capitalized in a paper written for a more general audience. Likewise, in some contexts it is not unusual to see the titles of certain powerful officials capitalized even when not accompanying a proper noun:

The President took few members of his staff to Camp David with him.

Colons

We all know certain uses for the colon. A colon can, for example, separate the parts of a statement of time (*4:25 A.M.*), separate chapter and verse in a biblical quotation (*John 3:16*), and close the salutation of a business letter (*Dear Senator Keaton:*). But the colon has other, less well-known uses that can add extra flexibility to sentence structure.

The colon can introduce into a sentence certain kinds of material, such as a list, a quotation, or a restatement or description of material mentioned earlier:

LIST

The committee's research proposal promised to do three things: (1) establish the extent of the problem, (2) examine several possible solutions, and (3) estimate the cost of each solution.

QUOTATION

In his speech, the mayor challenged us with these words: "How will your council's work make a difference in the life of our city?"

RESTATEMENT OR DESCRIPTION

Ahead of us, according to the senator's chief of staff, lay the biggest job of all: convincing our constituents of the plan's benefits.

Commas

The comma is perhaps the most troublesome of all marks of punctuation, no doubt because its use is governed by so many variables, such as sentence length, rhetorical emphasis, and changing notions of style. The most common problems are outlined below.

The Comma Splice

A *comma splice* is the joining of two complete sentences with only a comma:

An impeachment is merely an indictment of a government official, actual removal usually requires a vote by a legislative body.

An unemployed worker who has been effectively retrained is no longer an economic problem for the community, he has become an asset.

It might be possible for the city to assess fees on the sale of real estate, however, such a move would be criticized by the community of real estate developers.

In each of these passages, two complete sentences (also called *independent clauses*) have been spliced together by a comma, which is an inadequate break between the two sentences.

One foolproof way to check your paper for comma splices is to read the structures on both sides of each comma carefully. If you find a complete sentence on each side, and if the sentence following the comma does not begin with a coordinating conjunction (*and, but, for, nor, or, so, yet*), then you have found a comma splice.

Simply reading the draft to try to "hear" the comma splices may not work, because the rhetorical features of your prose—its "movement"—may make it hard to detect this kind of error in sentence completeness. There are five commonly used ways to correct comma splices:

1. Place a period between the two independent clauses:

   INCORRECT   A political candidate receives many benefits from his or her affiliation with a political party, there are liabilities as well.

   CORRECT   A political candidate receives many benefits from his or her affiliation with a political party. There are liabilities as well.

2. Place a comma and a coordinating conjunction (*and, but, for, or, nor, so, yet*) between the independent clauses:

INCORRECT	The councilman's speech described the major differences of opinion over the economic situation, it also suggested a possible course of action.
CORRECT	The councilman's speech described the major differences of opinion over the economic situation, and it also suggested a possible course of action.

3. Place a semicolon between the independent clauses:

INCORRECT	Some people feel that the federal government should play a large role in establishing a housing policy for the homeless, many others disagree.
CORRECT	Some people feel that the federal government should play a large role in establishing a housing policy for the homeless; many others disagree.

4. Rewrite the two clauses as one independent clause:

INCORRECT	Television ads played a big part in the campaign, however they were not the deciding factor in the challenger's victory over the incumbent.
CORRECT	Television ads played a large but not a decisive role in the challenger's victory over the incumbent.

5. Change one of the independent clauses into a dependent clause by beginning it with a subordinating word (*although, after, as, because, before, if, though, unless, when, which, where*), which prevents the clause from being able to stand on its own as a complete sentence.

INCORRECT	The election was held last Tuesday, there was a poor voter turnout.
CORRECT	When the election was held last Tuesday, there was a poor voter turnout.

Commas in a Compound Sentence

A *compound sentence* is composed of two or more independent clauses—two complete sentences. When these two clauses are joined by a coordinating conjunction, the conjunction should be preceded by a comma to signal the reader that another independent clause follows. (This is method number 2 for fixing a comma splice, described above.) When the comma is missing, the reader is not expecting to find the second half of a compound sentence and may be distracted from the text.

As the following examples indicate, the missing comma is especially a problem in longer sentences or in sentences in which other coordinating conjunctions appear. Notice how the comma sorts out the two main parts of the compound sentence, eliminating confusion:

INCORRECT   The senator promised to visit the hospital and investigate the problem and then he called the press conference to a close.

CORRECT   The senator promised to visit the hospital and investigate the problem, and then he called the press conference to a close.

INCORRECT   The water board can neither make policy nor enforce it nor can its members serve on auxiliary water committees.

CORRECT   The water board can neither make policy nor enforce it, nor can its members serve on auxiliary water committees.

An exception to this rule arises in shorter sentences, where the comma may not be necessary to make the meaning clear:

The mayor phoned and we thanked him for his support.

However, it is never wrong to place a comma after the conjunction between independent clauses. If you are the least bit unsure of your audience's notion of "proper" grammar, it is a good idea to take the conservative approach and use the comma:

The mayor phoned, and we thanked him for his support.

Commas with Restrictive and Nonrestrictive Elements

A *nonrestrictive element* is a part of a sentence—a word, phrase, or clause—that adds information about another element in the sentence without restricting or limiting its meaning. Although this information may be useful, the nonrestrictive element is not needed for the sentence to make sense. To signal its inessential nature, the nonrestrictive element is set off from the rest of the sentence with commas.

The failure to use commas to indicate the nonrestrictive nature of a sentence element can cause confusion. See, for example, how the presence or absence of commas affects our understanding of the following sentence:

The mayor was talking with the policeman, who won the outstanding service award last year.

The mayor was talking with the policeman who won the outstanding service award last year.

Can you see that the comma changes the meaning of the sentence? In the first version of the sentence, the comma makes the information that follows it incidental: *The mayor was talking with the policeman, who happens to have won the service award last year.* In the second version of the sentence, the information following the word *policeman* is vital to the sense of the sentence; it tells us specifically *which* policeman—presumably there are more than one—the mayor was addressing. Here the lack of a comma has transformed the material following the word *policeman* into a *restrictive element,* which means that it is necessary to our understanding of the sentence.

Be sure that you make a clear distinction in your paper between nonrestrictive and restrictive elements by setting off the nonrestrictive elements with commas.

Commas in a Series

A series is any two or more items of a similar nature that appear consecutively in a sentence. These items may be individual words, phrases, or clauses. In a series of three or more items, the items are separated by commas:

> *The senator, the mayor, and the police chief* all attended the ceremony.

> Because of the new zoning regulations, *all trailer parks must be moved out of the neighborhood, all small businesses must apply for recertification and tax status, and the two local churches must repave their parking lots.*

The final comma in the series, the one before *and,* is sometimes left out, especially in newspaper writing. This practice, however, can make for confusion, especially in longer, complicated sentences like the second example above. Here is the way this sentence would read without the final, or serial, comma:

> Because of the new zoning regulations, all trailer parks must be moved out of the neighborhood, all small businesses must apply for recertification and tax status and the two local churches must repave their parking lots.

Notice that, without a comma, the division between the second and third items in the series is not clear. This is the sort of ambiguous structure that can cause a reader to backtrack and lose concentration. You can avoid such confusion by always using that final comma. Remember, however, that if you do decide to include it, do so consistently; make sure it appears in every series in your paper.

Dangling Modifiers

A *modifier* is a word or group of words used to describe, or modify, another word in the sentence. A *dangling modifier* appears at either the beginning or the end of a sentence and seems to be describing some word other than the one the writer obviously intended. The modifier therefore "dangles," disconnected from its correct meaning. It is often hard for the writer to spot a dangling modifier, but readers can—and will—find them, and the result can be disastrous for the sentence, as the following examples demonstrate:

INCORRECT	Flying low over Washington, the White House was seen.
CORRECT	Flying low over Washington, we saw the White House.
INCORRECT	Worried at the cost of the program, sections of the bill were trimmed in committee.
CORRECT	Worried at the cost of the program, the committee trimmed sections of the bill.
INCORRECT	To lobby for prison reform, a lot of effort went into the television ads.
CORRECT	The lobby group put a lot of effort into the television ads advocating prison reform.

INCORRECT   Stunned, the television broadcast the defeated senator's concession speech.

CORRECT   The television broadcast the stunned senator's concession speech.

Note that, in the first two incorrect sentences above, the confusion is largely due to the use of *passive-voice* verbs: "the White House *was seen*," "sections of the bill *were trimmed*." Often, although not always, a dangling modifier results because the actor in the sentence—*we* in the first sentence, *the committee* in the second—is either distanced from the modifier or obliterated by the passive-voice verb. It is a good idea to avoid using the passive voice unless you have a specific reason for doing so.

One way to check for dangling modifiers is to examine all modifiers at the beginning or end of your sentences. Look especially for *to be* phrases or for words ending in *-ing* or *-ed* at the start of the modifier. Then see if the modified word is close enough to the phrase to be properly connected.

Parallelism

Series of two or more words, phrases, or clauses within a sentence should have the same grammatical structure, a situation called *parallelism*. Parallel structures can add power and balance to your writing by creating a strong rhetorical rhythm. Here is a famous example of parallelism from the Preamble to the U.S. Constitution. (The capitalization follows that of the original eighteenth-century document. Parallel structures have been italicized:)

> We the People of the United States, in Order to *form a more perfect Union, Establish justice, insure Domestic Tranquillity, provide for the common defense, promote the general Welfare,* and *secure the Blessings of Liberty to ourselves and our Posterity,* do *ordain* and *establish* this Constitution for the United States of America.

There are actually two series in this sentence: the first, composed of six phrases, each of which completes the infinitive phrase beginning with the word to (*to form, [to] Establish, [to] insure, [to] provide, [to] promote,* and *[to] secure*); the second, consisting of two verbs (*ordain* and *establish*). These parallel series appeal to our love of balance and pattern, and give an authoritative tone to the sentence. The writer, we feel, has thought long and carefully about the matter at hand and has taken firm control of it.

Because we find a special satisfaction in balanced structures, we are more likely to remember ideas phrased in parallelisms than in less highly ordered language. For this reason, as well as for the sense of authority and control that they suggest, parallel structures are common in political utterances:

> We hold these truths to be self-evident, that all men are created equal, that they are endowed by their Creator with certain unalienable rights, that among these are life, liberty, and the pursuit of happiness.
> —The Declaration of Independence, 1776

> But in a larger sense, we cannot dedicate, we cannot consecrate, we cannot hallow this ground. The brave men, living and dead, who struggled here, have consecrated it far above our poor power to add or detract. The world

will little note, nor long remember what we say here; but it can never forget what they did here.

—Abraham Lincoln, Gettysburg Address, 1863

Ask not what your country can do for you, ask what you can do for your country.

—John F. Kennedy, Inaugural Address, 1961

Faulty Parallelism

If the parallelism of a passage is not carefully maintained, the writing can seem sloppy and out of balance. Scan your writing to make sure that all series and lists have parallel structure. The following examples show how to correct faulty parallelism:

INCORRECT	The mayor promises not only *to reform* the police department but also *the giving of raises* to all city employees. [Connective structures such as *not only . . . but also* and *both . . . and* introduce elements that should be parallel.]
CORRECT	The mayor promises not only *to reform* the police department but also *to give* raises to all city employees.
INCORRECT	The cost *of doing nothing* is greater than the cost *to renovate* the apartment block.
CORRECT	The cost *of doing nothing* is greater than the cost *of renovating* the apartment block.
INCORRECT	Here are the items on the committee's agenda: (1) *to discuss* the new property tax; (2) *to revise* the wording of the city charter; (3) *a vote* on the city manager's request for an assistant.
CORRECT	Here are the items on the committee's agenda: (1) *to discuss* the new property tax; (2) *to revise* the wording of the city charter; (3) *to vote* on the city manager's request for an assistant.

Fused (Run-on) Sentences

A *fused sentence* is one in which two or more independent clauses (passages that can stand as complete sentences) have been run together without the aid of any suitable connecting word, phrase, or punctuation. There are several ways to correct a fused sentence:

INCORRECT	The council members were exhausted they had debated for two hours.
CORRECT	The council members were exhausted. They had debated for two hours. [The clauses have been separated into two sentences.]
CORRECT	The council members were exhausted; they had debated for two hours. [The clauses have been separated by a semicolon.]

CORRECT	The council members were exhausted, having debated for two hours. [The second clause has been rephrased as a dependent clause.]
INCORRECT	Our policy analysis impressed the committee it also convinced them to reconsider their action.
CORRECT	Our policy analysis impressed the committee and also convinced them to reconsider their action. [The second clause has been rephrased as part of the first clause.]
CORRECT	Our policy analysis impressed the committee, and it also convinced them to reconsider their action. [The clauses have been separated by a comma and a coordinating word.]

Although a fused sentence is easily noticeable to the reader, it can be maddeningly difficult for the writer to catch. Unpracticed writers tend to read through the fused spots, sometimes supplying the break that is usually heard when sentences are spoken. To check for fused sentences, read the independent clauses in your paper carefully, making sure that there are adequate breaks among all of them.

Pronoun Errors

Its Versus *It's*

Do not make the mistake of trying to form the possessive of *it* in the same way that you form the possessive of most nouns. The pronoun *it* shows possession by simply adding an *s*.

The prosecuting attorney argued the case on *its* merits.

The word *it's* is a contraction of *it is:*

It's the most expensive program ever launched by the council.

What makes the *its/it's* rule so confusing is that most nouns form the singular possessive by adding an apostrophe and an *s:*

The jury's verdict startled the crowd.

When proofreading, any time you come to the word *it's*, substitute the phrase *it is* while you read. If the phrase makes sense, you have used the correct form. If you have used the word *it's,*

The newspaper article was misleading in *it's* analysis of the election.

then read it as *it is:*

The newspaper article was misleading in *it is* analysis of the election.

If the phrase makes no sense, substitute *its* for *it's:*

The newspaper article was misleading in *its* analysis of the election.

Vague Pronoun References

Pronouns are words that take the place of nouns or other pronouns that have already been mentioned in your writing. The most common pronouns include *he, she, it, they, them, those, which,* and *who.* You must make sure there is no confusion about the word to which each pronoun refers:

> The mayor said that *he* would support our bill if the city council would also back it.

The word that the pronoun replaces is called its *antecedent.* To check the accuracy of your pronoun references, ask yourself, "To what does the pronoun refer?" Then answer the question carefully, making sure that there is not more than one possible antecedent. Consider the following example:

> Several special interest groups decided to defeat the new health care bill. *This* became the turning point of the government's reform campaign.

To what does the word *This* refer? The immediate answer seems to be the word *bill* at the end of the previous sentence. It is more likely that the writer was referring to the attempt of the special interest groups to defeat the bill, but there is no word in the first sentence that refers specifically to this action. The pronoun reference is thus unclear. One way to clarify the reference is to change the beginning of the second sentence:

> Several special *interest groups* decided to defeat the new health care bill. *Their attack on the bill* became the turning point of the government's reform campaign.

This point is further demonstrated by the following sentence:

> When John F. Kennedy appointed his brother Robert to the position of U.S. attorney general, *he* had little idea how widespread the corruption in the Teamsters Union was.

To whom does the word *he* refer? It is unclear whether the writer is referring to John or Robert Kennedy. One way to clarify the reference is simply to repeat the antecedent instead of using a pronoun:

> When John F. Kennedy appointed his brother Robert to the position of U.S. attorney general, Robert had little idea how widespread the corruption in the Teamsters Union was.

Pronoun Agreement

A pronoun must agree with its antecedent in both gender and number, as the following examples demonstrate:

> Mayor Smith said that *he* appreciated our club's support in the election.

> One reporter asked the senator what *she* would do if the president offered *her* a cabinet post.

Having listened to our case, the judge decided to rule on *it* within the week.

Engineers working on the housing project said *they* were pleased with the renovation so far.

Certain words, however, can be troublesome antecedents, because they may look like plural pronouns but are actually singular:

| anyone | each | either | everybody | everyone |
| nobody | no one | somebody | someone | |

A pronoun referring to one of these words in a sentence must be singular too:

INCORRECT   *Each* of the women in the support group brought *their* children.

CORRECT   *Each* of the women in the support group brought *her* children.

INCORRECT   *Has* everybody received *their* ballot?

CORRECT   *Has* everybody received *his or her* ballot? [The two gender-specific pronouns are used to avoid sexist language.]

CORRECT   Have *all the delegates* received *their* ballots? [The singular antecedent has been changed to a plural one.]

A Shift in Person

It is important to avoid shifting unnecessarily among first person (*I, we*), second person (*you*), and third person (*she, he, it, one, they*). Such shifts can cause confusion:

INCORRECT   *Most people* [third person] who run for office find that if *you* [second person] tell the truth during *your* campaign, *you* will gain the voters' respect.

CORRECT   *Most people* who run for office find that if *they* tell the truth during *their* campaigns, *they* will gain the voters' respect.

INCORRECT   *One* [first person] cannot tell whether *they* [third person] are suited for public office until *they* decide to run.

CORRECT   *One* cannot tell whether *one* is suited for public office until *one* decides to run.

Quotation Marks

It can be difficult to remember when to use quotation marks and where they go in relation to other punctuation. When faced with these questions, unpracticed writers often try to rely on logic rather than on a rule book, but the rules do not always seem to rely on logic. The only way to make sure of your use of quotation marks is to memorize the rules. Luckily, there are not many.

The Use of Quotation Marks

Use quotation marks to enclose direct quotations that are not longer than four typed lines:

> In his farewell address to the American people, George Washington warned, "The great rule of conduct for us, in regard to foreign nations, is, in extending our commercial relations, to have with them as little political connection as possible." (Washington 1991, S. Doc. 3)

Longer quotes are placed in a double-spaced block, *without* quotation marks:

> Lincoln clearly explained his motive for continuing the Civil War in his August 22, 1862, response to Horace Greeley's open letter:
>
>> I would save the Union. I would save it the shortest way under the Constitution. The sooner the National authority can be restored, the nearer the Union will be the Union as it was. If there be those who would not save the Union unless they could at the same time save Slavery, I do not agree with them. If there be those who would not save the Union unless they could at the same time destroy Slavery, I do not agree with them. (Lincoln 1946, 652)

Use single quotation marks to set off quotations within quotations:

> "I intend," said the senator, "to use in my speech a line from Frost's poem, 'The Road Not Taken.'"

NOTE. When the quote occurs at the end of the sentence, both the single and double quotation marks are placed outside the period.

Use quotation marks to set off titles of the following:

> Short poems (those not printed as a separate volume)
> Short stories
> Articles or essays
> Songs
> Episodes of television or radio shows

Use quotation marks to set off words or phrases used in special ways:

1. To convey irony:

   The "liberal" administration has done nothing but cater to big business.

2. To indicate a technical term:

   To "filibuster" is to delay legislation, usually through prolonged speech-making. The last notable filibuster occurred just last week in the Senate. [Once the term is defined, it is not placed in quotation marks again.]

Quotation Marks in Relation to Other Punctuation

Place commas and periods *inside* closing quotation marks:

> "My fellow Americans," said the president, "there are tough times ahead of us."

Place colons and semicolons *outside* closing quotation marks:

> In his speech on voting, the governor warned against "an encroaching in-dolence"; he was referring to the middle class.

> There are several victims of the government's campaign to "Turn Back the Clock": the homeless, the elderly, the mentally impaired.

Use the context to determine whether to place question marks, exclamation points, and dashes inside or outside closing quotation marks. If the punctuation is part of the quotation, place it inside the quotation mark:

> "When will Congress make up its mind?" asked the ambassador.
> The demonstrators shouted, "Free the hostages!" and "No more slavery!"

If the punctuation is not part of the quotation, place it outside the quotation mark:

> Which president said, "We have nothing to fear but fear itself"? [Although the quote is a complete sentence, you do not place a period after it. There can only be one piece of terminal punctuation, or punctuation that ends a sentence.]

Semicolons

The semicolon is a little-used punctuation mark that you should learn to in-corporate into your writing strategy because of its many potential applications. For example, a semicolon can be used to correct a comma splice:

INCORRECT   The union representatives left the meeting in good spirits, their demands were met.

CORRECT   The union representatives left the meeting in good spirits; their demands were met.

INCORRECT   Several guests at the fundraiser had lost their invitations, how-ever, we were able to seat them anyway.

CORRECT   Several guests at the fundraiser had lost their invitations; how-ever, we were able to seat them anyway. [Conjunctive adverbs such as *however, therefore,* and *thus* are not coordinating words (such as *and, but, or, for, so, yet*) and cannot be used with a comma to link independent clauses. If the second independent clause begins with *however,* it must be preceded by either a period or a semicolon.]

As you can see from the second example above, connecting two independent clauses with a semicolon instead of a period strengthens their relationship.

Semicolons can also separate items in a series when the series items them-selves contain commas:

> The newspaper account of the rally stressed the march, which drew the biggest crowd; the mayor's speech, which drew tremendous applause; and the party in the park, which lasted for hours.

Avoid misusing semicolons. For example, use a comma, not a semicolon, to separate an independent clause from a dependent clause:

INCORRECT   Students from the college volunteered to answer phones during the pledge drive; which was set up to generate money for the new arts center.

CORRECT   Students from the college volunteered to answer phones during the pledge drive, which was set up to generate money for the new arts center.

Do not overuse semicolons. Although they are useful, too many semicolons in your writing can distract your readers' attention. Avoid monotony by using semicolons sparingly.

Sentence Fragments

A *fragment* is an incomplete part of a sentence that is punctuated and capitalized as if it were an entire sentence. It is an especially disruptive error, because it obscures the connections that the words of a sentence must make in order to complete the reader's understanding.

Students sometimes write fragments because they are concerned that a sentence needs to be shortened. Remember that cutting the length of a sentence merely by adding a period somewhere often creates a fragment. When checking writing for fragments, it is essential that you read each sentence carefully to determine whether it has (1) a complete subject and a verb; and (2) a subordinating word before the subject and verb, which makes the construction a subordinate clause rather than a complete sentence.

Types of Sentence Fragments

Some fragments lack a verb:

INCORRECT   The chairperson of our committee, having received a letter from the mayor. [The word *having*, which can be used as a verb, is here being used as a gerund introducing a participial phrase. Watch out for words that look like verbs but are being used in another way.]

CORRECT   The chairperson of our committee received a letter from the mayor.

Some fragments lack a subject:

INCORRECT   Our study shows that there is broad support for improvement in the health care system. And in the unemployment system.

CORRECT   Our study shows that there is broad support for improvement in the health care system and in the unemployment system.

Some fragments are subordinate clauses:

INCORRECT   After the latest edition of the newspaper came out. [This clause has the two major components of a complete sentence: a subject (*edition*) and a verb (*came*). Indeed, if the first word (*After*) were deleted, the clause would be a complete sentence. But that first word is a *subordinating word,* which prevents the following clause from standing on its own as a complete sentence. Watch out for this kind of construction. It is called a *subordinate clause,* and it is not a sentence.]

CORRECT   After the latest edition of the newspaper came out, the mayor's press secretary was overwhelmed with phone calls. [A common method of correcting a subordinate clause that has been punctuated as a complete sentence is to connect it to the complete sentence to which it is closest in meaning.]

INCORRECT   Several representatives asked for copies of the vice president's position paper. Which called for reform of the Environmental Protection Agency.

CORRECT   Several representatives asked for copies of the vice president's position paper, which called for reform of the Environmental Protection Agency.

Spelling

All of us have problems spelling certain words that we have not yet committed to memory. But most writers are not as bad at spelling as they believe they are. Usually an individual finds only a handful of words troubling. It is important to be as sensitive as possible to your own particular spelling problems—and to keep a dictionary handy. There is no excuse for failing to check spelling.

What follows are a list of commonly confused words and a list of commonly misspelled words. Read through the lists, looking for those words that tend to give you trouble. If you have any questions, consult your dictionary.

COMMONLY CONFUSED WORDS

accept/except	complement/compliment	fair/fare
advice/advise	conscience/conscious	formally/formerly
affect/effect	corps/corpse	forth/fourth
aisle/isle	council/counsel	hear/here
allusion/illusion	dairy/diary	heard/herd
an/and	descent/dissent	hole/whole
angel/angle	desert/dessert	human/humane
ascent/assent	device/devise	its/it's
bare/bear	die/dye	know/no
brake/break	dominant/dominate	later/latter
breath/breathe	elicit/illicit	lay/lie
buy/by	eminent/immanent/	lead/led
capital/capitol	imminent	lessen/lesson
choose/chose	envelop/envelope	loose/lose
cite/sight/site	every day/everyday	may be/maybe

miner/minor	raise/raze	threw/through
moral/morale	reality/realty	too/to/two
of/off	respectfully/respectively	track/tract
passed/past	reverend/reverent	waist/waste
patience/patients	right/rite/write	waive/wave
peace/piece	road/rode	weak/week
personal/personnel	scene/seen	weather/whether
plain/plane precede/	sense/since	were/where
proceed	stationary/stationery	which/witch
presence/presents	straight/strait	whose/who's
principal/principle	taught/taut	your/you're
quiet/quite	than/then	
rain/reign/rein	their/there/they're	

COMMONLY MISSPELLED WORDS

acceptable	easily	irresistible
accessible	efficient	irritate
accommodate	environment	knowledge
accompany	equipped	license
accustomed	exceed	likelihood
acquire	exercise	maintenance
against	existence	manageable
annihilate	experience	meanness
apparent	fascinate	mischievous
arguing	finally	missile
argument	foresee	necessary
authentic	forty	nevertheless
before	fulfill	no one
begin	gauge	noticeable
beginning	guaranteed	noticing
believe	guard	nuisance
benefited	harass	occasion
bulletin	hero	occasionally
business	heroes	occurred
cannot	humorous	occurrences
category	hurried	omission
committee	hurriedly	omit
condemn	hypocrite	opinion
courteous	ideally	opponent
definitely	immediately	parallel
dependent	immense	parole
desperate	incredible	peaceable
develop	innocuous	performance
different	intercede	pertain
disappear	interrupt	practical
disappoint	irrelevant	preparation

probably	rhythm	successfully
process	ridiculous	susceptible
professor	roommate	suspicious
prominent	satellite	technical
pronunciation	scarcity	temporary
psychology	scenery	tendency
publicly	science	therefore
pursue	secede	tragedy
pursuing	secession	truly
questionnaire	secretary	tyranny
realize	senseless	unanimous
receipt	separate	unconscious
received	sergeant	undoubtedly
recession	shining	until
recommend	significant	vacuum
referring	sincerely	valuable
religious	skiing	various
remembrance	stubbornness	vegetable
reminisce	studying	visible
repetition	succeed	without
representative	success	women

◆ CHAPTER 3 ◆
Paper Formats

Your format makes your paper's first impression. Justly or not, accurately or not, it announces your professional competence—or lack of competence. A well-executed format implies that your paper is worth reading. More importantly, however, a proper format brings information to your readers in a familiar form that has the effect of setting their minds at ease. Your paper's format should therefore impress your readers with your academic competence as a political scientist by following accepted professional standards. Like the style and clarity of your writing, your format communicates messages that are often more readily and profoundly received than the content of the document itself.

The formats described in this chapter are in conformance with generally accepted standards in the discipline of political science, including instructions for the following elements:

General page formats   Table of contents
Title page   Reference page
Abstract   List of tables and figures
Executive summary   Text
Outline page   Appendixes

Except for special instructions from your instructor, follow the directions in this manual exactly.

3.1 GENERAL PAGE FORMATS

Political science assignments should be printed on $8\frac{1}{2}$-by-11-inch premium white bond paper, 20 pound or heavier. Do not use any other size or color except to comply with special instructions from your instructor, and do not use off-white or poor quality (draft) paper. Political science that is worth the time to write and read is worth good paper.

Always submit to your instructor an original typed or computer-printed manuscript. Do not submit a photocopy! Always make a second paper copy and back up your electronic copy for your own files in case the original is lost.

Margins, except in theses and dissertations, should be one inch on all sides of the paper. Unless otherwise instructed, all papers should be *double-spaced* in a 12-point word-processing font or typewriter pica type. Typewriter elite type may be used if another is not available. Select a font that is plain and easy to read, such as Helvetica, Courier, Garamond, or Times Roman. Do not use script, stylized, or elaborate fonts.

Page numbers should appear in the upper right-hand corner of each page, starting immediately after the title page. No page number should appear on the title page or on the first page of the text. Page numbers should appear one inch from the right side and one-half inch from the top of the page. They should proceed consecutively beginning with the title page (although the first number is not actually printed on the title page). You may use lowercase roman numerals (i, ii, iii, iv, v, vi, vii, viii, ix, x, and so on) for the pages, such as the title page, table of contents, and table of figures, that precede the first page of text, but if you use them, the numbers must be placed at the center of the bottom of the page.

Ask your instructor about bindings. In the absence of further directions, *do not bind* your paper or enclose it within a plastic cover sheet. Place one staple in the upper left-hand corner, or use a paper clip at the top of the paper. Note that a paper to be submitted to a journal for publication should not be clipped, stapled, or bound in any form.

Title Page

The following information will be centered on the title page:

Title of the paper
Name of writer
Course name, section number, and instructor
College or university
Date

```
                    The Second Bush Presidency

                              by

                  Nicole Ashley Linscheid



                  The American Presidency

                           POL213

                  Dr. Bushrod Collyflour

                  St. Johnswort College

                      January 1, 2006
```

As the sample title page shows, the title should clearly describe the problem addressed in the paper. If the paper discusses juvenile recidivism in Albemarle County jails, for example, the title "Recidivism in the Albemarle County Criminal Justice System" is professional, clear, and helpful to the reader. "Albemarle County," "Juvenile Justice," or "County Jails" are all too vague to be effective. Also, the title should not be "cute." A cute title may attract attention for a play on Broadway, but it will detract from the credibility of a paper in political science. "Inadequate Solid Waste Disposal Facilities in Denver" is professional. "Down in the Dumps" is not.

In addition, title pages for position papers and policy analysis papers must include the name, title, and organization of the public official who has the authority and responsibility to implement the recommendation of your paper. The person to whom you address the paper should be the person who has the responsibility and the authority to make the decision that is called for in your paper. The "address" should include the person's name, title, and organization, as shown in the example of a title page for a position paper that follows. To identify the appropriate official, first carefully define the problem and the best solution. Then ascertain the person or persons who have the authority to solve the problem. If you recommend installation of a traffic signal at a particular intersection, for example, find out who makes the decisions regarding such actions in your community. It may be the public safety director, a transportation planning commission, or a town council.

```
          Oak City Police Department Personnel Policy Revisions



                              submitted to



                          Farley Z. Simmons

                         Director of Personnel

                          Police Department

                         Oak City, Arkansas



                                  by



                        Luke Tyler Linscheid

                   American National Government

                             GOV 1001

                        Dr. Prospect Pigeon

                   Perpetual Homework University

                          January 21, 2006
```

Abstract

An abstract is a brief summary of a paper written primarily to allow potential readers to see if the paper contains information of sufficient interest for them to read. People conducting research want specific kinds of information, and they often read dozens of abstracts looking for papers that contain relevant data. Abstracts have the designation "Abstract" centered near the top of the page. Next is the title, also centered, followed by a paragraph that precisely states the paper's topic, research and analysis methods, and results and conclusions. The abstract should be written in one paragraph of no more than 150 words. Remember, an abstract is not an introduction; instead, it is a summary, as demonstrated in the sample below.

Abstract

Bertrand Russell's View of Mysticism

This paper reviews Bertrand Russell's writings on religion, mysticism, and science, and defines his perspective of the contribution of mysticism to scientific knowledge. Russell drew a sharp distinction between what he considered to be (1) the essence of religion, and (2) dogma or assertions attached to religion by theologians and religious leaders. Although some of his writings, including *Why I Am Not a Christian,* appear hostile to all aspects of religion, Russell actually asserts that religion, freed from doctrinal encumbrances, not only fulfills certain psychological needs but evokes many of the most beneficial human impulses. He believes that religious mysticism generates an intellectual disinterestedness that may be useful to science, but that it is not a source of a special type of knowledge beyond investigation by science.

Executive Summary

An executive summary, like an abstract, summarizes the content of a paper but does so in more detail. A sample executive summary is given on page 51. Whereas abstracts are read by people who are doing research, executive summaries are more likely to be read by people who need some or all of the information in the paper in order to make a decision. Many people, however, will read the executive summary to fix clearly in their mind the organization and results of a paper before reading the paper itself.

Executive Summary

Municipal parks in Springfield are deteriorating because of inadequate maintenance, and one park in particular, Oak Ridge Community Park, needs immediate attention. The problem is that parking, picnic, and restroom facilities at Oak Ridge Community Park have deteriorated as a result of normal wear, adverse weather, and vandalism, and are inadequate to meet public demand. The park was established as a public recreation "Class B" facility in 1967. Only one major renovation has occurred: in the summer of 1987 general building repair was done, and new swing sets were installed. The Park Department estimates that 10,000 square feet of new parking space, fourteen items of playground equipment, seventeen new picnic tables, and repairs on current facilities would cost about $43,700.

Three possible solutions have been given extensive consideration in this paper. One option is to do nothing. Area residents will use the area less as deterioration continues, but no immediate outlay of public funds will be necessary. The first alternative solution is to make all repairs immediately. Area residents will enjoy immediate and increased use of facilities. Taxpayers have turned down the last three tax increase requests. Revenue bonds may be acceptable to a total of $20,000, according to the City Manager, but no more than $5,000 per year is available from general city revenues.

A second alternative is to make repairs, according to a priority list, over a five-year period, using a combination of general city revenues and a $20,000 first-year bond issue that will require City Council and voter approval. Residents will enjoy the most needed improvements immediately.

The recommendation of this report is that the second alternative be adopted by the City Council. The City Council should, during its May 15 meeting, (1) adopt a resolution of intent to commit $5,000 per year for five years from the general revenue fund, dedicated to this purpose; and (2) approve for submission to public vote in the November 2007 election a $20,000 bond issue.

Outline Page

An outline page is a specific type of executive summary. Most often found in position papers and policy analysis papers, an outline page provides more information about the organization of the paper than does an executive summary. The outline shows clearly the sections in the paper and the information in each. An outline page is an asset because it allows busy decision-makers to understand the entire content of a paper without reading it all or to refer quickly to a specific part for more information. Position papers and policy analysis papers are written for people in positions of authority who normally need to make a variety of decisions in a short period. Outline pages reduce the amount of time they need to understand a policy problem, the alternative solutions, and the author's preferred solution. Outline pages sequentially list the complete topic sentences of the major paragraphs of a paper, in outline form. In a position paper, for example, you will be stating a problem, defining possible solutions, and then recommending the best solution. These three steps will be the major headings in your outline. (See Chapter 1 for instructions on writing an outline.) Wait until you have completed the paper before writing the outline page. Take the topic sentences from the leading (most important) paragraph in each section of your paper and place them in the appropriate places in your outline. A sample outline page is given on page 53.

Table of Contents

A table of contents does not provide as much information as an outline, but it does include the titles of the major divisions and subdivisions of a paper. Tables of contents are not normally required in student papers or papers presented at professional meetings but may be included. They are normally required, however, in books, theses, and dissertations. The table of contents should consist of the chapter or main section titles, and the headings used in the text, with one additional level of titles, along with their page numbers, as the sample on page 54 demonstrates.

Reference Page

The format for references is discussed in detail in Chapter 4. Sample reference pages for two formats, the author-date system and the documentary-note system, appear in Chapter 4.

3.2   TABLES, ILLUSTRATIONS, FIGURES, AND APPENDIXES

List of Tables, Illustrations, and Figures

A list of tables, illustrations, or figures contains their titles as used in the paper, in the order in which they appear, along with their page numbers. You

Outline of Contents

I. The problem is that parking, picnic, and restroom facilities at Oak Ridge Community Park have deteriorated as a result of normal wear, adverse weather, and vandalism, and are inadequate to meet public demand.
    A. Only one major renovation has occurred since 1967, when the park was opened.
    B. The Park Department estimates that 10,000 square feet of new parking space, fourteen items of playground equipment, seventeen new picnic tables, and repairs on current facilities would cost about $43,700.
II. Three possible solutions have been given extensive consideration:
    A. One option is to do nothing. Area residents will use the area less as deterioration continues, but no immediate outlay of public funds will be necessary.
    B. The first alternative solution is to make all repairs immediately. Area residents will enjoy immediate and increased use of facilities. $43,700 in funds will be needed. Sources include: (1) Community Development Block Grant funds; (2) increased property taxes; (3) revenue bonds; and (4) general city revenues.
    C. A second alternative is to make repairs according to a priority list over a five–year period, using a combination of general city revenues and a $20,000 first-year bond issue. Residents will enjoy the most needed improvements immediately. The bond issue will require City Council and voter approval.
III. The recommendation of this report is that alternative C be adopted by the City Council. The benefit/cost analysis demonstrates that residents will be satisfied if basic improvements are made immediately. The City Council should, during its May 15 meeting, (1) adopt a resolution of intent to commit $5,000 per year for five years from the general revenue fund, dedicated to this purpose; and (2) approve for submission to public vote in the November 2007 election a $20,000 bond issue.

Contents

may list tables, illustrations, and figures together under the title "Figures" (and call them all "Figures" in the text), or if you have more than a half page of entries, you may have separate lists for tables, illustrations, and figures (and title them accordingly in the text). An example of the format for such lists is below.

Figures

Tables

Tables are used in the text to show relationships among data, to help the reader come to a conclusion or understand a certain point. Tables that show simple results or "raw" data should be placed in an appendix. Tables should not reiterate the content of the text. They should say something new, and they should stand on their own. In other words, the reader should be able to understand the table without reading the text. Clearly label the columns and rows in the table. Each word in the title (except articles, prepositions, and conjunctions) should be capitalized. The source of the information should be shown immediately below the table, not in a footnote or endnote. A sample table is shown below.

Table 1. Projections of the Total Population of Selected States, 2005 to 2035 (in thousands)

State	2005	2015	2025	2030	2035
Alabama	4,253	4,451	4,631	4,956	5,224
Illinois	11,830	12,051	12,266	12,808	13,440
Maine	1,241	1,259	1,285	1,362	1,423
New Mexico	1,605	1,860	2,016	2,300	2,612
Oklahoma	3,278	3,373	3,491	3,789	4,057
Tennessee	5,256	5,657	5,966	6,365	6,665
Virginia	6,618	6,997	7,324	7,921	8,466

Source: U.S. Census Bureau.

Illustrations and Figures

Illustrations are not normally inserted in the text of a political science paper, even in an appendix, unless they are necessary to explain the content. If illustrations are necessary, do not paste or tape photocopies of photographs or similar materials to the text or the appendix. Instead, photocopy each one on a separate sheet of paper and center it, along with its typed title, within the normal margins of the paper. The format of illustration titles should be the same as that for tables and figures.

Figures in the form of charts and graphs may be very helpful in presenting certain types of information, as the example shows on page 56.

Population Growth in Six States 2005 to 2035

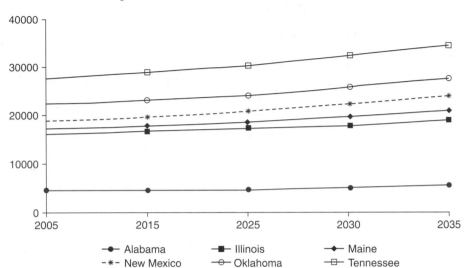

Appendixes

Appendixes are reference materials provided for the convenience of the reader at the back of the paper, after the text. Providing information that supplements the important facts in the text, they may include maps, charts, tables, and selected documents. Do not place materials that are merely interesting or decorative in your appendix. Use only items that will answer questions raised by the text or are necessary to explain the text. Follow the guidelines for formats for tables, illustrations, and figures when adding material in an appendix. At the top center of the page, label your first appendix "Appendix A," your second appendix "Appendix B," and so on. Do not append an entire government report, journal article, or other publication, but only the portions of such documents that are necessary to support your paper. The source of the information should always be evident on the appended pages.

3.3 TEXT

Ask your instructor for the number of pages required for the paper you are writing. The text should follow the directions explained in Chapters 1 and 2 of this manual and should conform to the format of the facsimile page shown on page 57.

Chapter Headings

Your paper should include no more than three levels of headings:

1. *Primary,* which should be centered, with each word except articles, prepositions, and conjunctions capitalized

Sample Passage of Text

> The problem is that parking, picnic, and restroom facilities at Oak Ridge Community Park have deteriorated as a result of normal wear, adverse weather, and vandalism, and are of inadequate quantity to meet public demand. The paved parking lot has crumbled and eroded. As many as two hundred cars park on the lawn during major holidays. Only one of the five swing sets is in safe operating condition. Each set accommodates four children, but during weekends and holidays many children wait turns for the available sets. Spray paint vandalism has marred the rest room facilities, which are inadequate to meet major holiday demands.
>
> The Department of Parks and Recreation established the park as a public recreation Class B facility in 1963. In the summer of 1987 the department conducted general building repair and installed new steel swing sets. Only minimal annual maintenance has occurred since that time.
>
> The department estimates that 10,000 square feet of new parking lot space, fourteen items of playground equipment, seventeen new picnic tables, and repairs on current facilities would cost about $43,700 (Department of Parks and Recreation 2005). Parking lot improvements include a new surface of coarse gravel on the old paved lot and expansion of the new paved lot by 10,000 square feet. The State Engineering Office estimates the cost of parking lot improvements to be $16,200.

2. *Secondary,* which begin at the left margin, also with each word except articles, prepositions, and conjunctions capitalized
3. *Tertiary,* which should be written in sentence style (with only the first word and proper nouns capitalized), with a period at the end, underlined

The following illustration shows the proper use of chapter headings:

The House of Representatives	(Primary Heading)
Impeachment Procedures of the House	(Secondary Heading)
<u>Rules for debate in impeachment proceedings</u>	(Tertiary Heading)

◆ CHAPTER 4 ◆
Citing Sources

4.1 THE APSA AUTHOR-DATE SYSTEM

One of your most important jobs as a research writer is to document your use of source material carefully and clearly. Failure to do so will cause your reader confusion, damage the effectiveness of your paper, and perhaps make you vulnerable to a charge of plagiarism. Proper documentation is more than just good form. It is a powerful indicator of your own commitment to scholarship and the sense of authority that you bring to your writing. Good documentation demonstrates your expertise as a researcher and increases your reader's trust in you and your work.

Unfortunately, as anybody who has ever written a research paper knows, getting the documentation right can be a frustrating, confusing job, especially for the writer who is not familiar with the citation system. Positioning each element of a single reference citation accurately can require a lot of time looking through the style manual. Even before you begin to work on the specific citations, there are important questions of style and format to answer.

What to Document

You must always credit direct quotes, as well as certain kinds of paraphrased material. Information that is basic—important dates, universally acknowledged facts or commonly held opinions—need not be cited. Information that is not widely known, however, should receive documentation. This type of material includes ideas, evaluations, critiques, and descriptions original to your source.

What if you are unsure whether a certain fact is an academic "given" or sufficiently unique to warrant attribution to your source? You are, after all, probably a newcomer to the field in which you are conducting your research. If in doubt, supply the documentation. It is better to overdocument than to fail to do justice to a source.

The Choice of Style

Whereas the question of which documentation style to use may be decided for you by your instructor, others may allow you a choice. There are several styles available, each designed to meet the needs of researchers in particular fields. The reference systems approved by the Modern Language Association (MLA) and the American Psychological Association (APA) are often used in the humanities and the social sciences and could serve the needs of the political science writer, but this manual offers the style most likely to be appropriate for political science papers: the APSA Author-Date System.

The American Political Science Association (APSA) has adopted a modification of the style elaborated in the *Chicago Manual of Style* (*CMS*), perhaps the most universally approved of all documentation authorities. One of the advantages of using the APSA style, which is outlined in an APSA pamphlet entitled *Style Manual for Political Science* (1993, revised 2005), is that it is designed to guide the professional political scientist in preparing a manuscript for submission to the *American Political Science Review*, the journal of the American Political Science Association and the most influential political science journal in publication. Learning the APSA documentation style, then, offers you as a student another crucial connection to the world of the political scientist. For this reason, there are models below of formats described in the APSA *Style Manual* in addition to other models found only in the *CMS*.

NOTE. The APSA *Style Manual* for Political Science covers only certain basic reference and bibliographical models. For other models and for more detailed suggestions about referencing format, the 2005 revised edition of the APSA *Style Manual* refers readers to the "latest edition" of the *CMS*, which in 2005 was the fifteenth (2003). The formats below are based on APSA guidelines, whenever such guidelines are available. Otherwise, the formats follow models taken from the fifteenth (2003) edition of the *CMS*, and, when necessary, from the more exhaustive fourteenth (1993) edition. Models based on the *CMS* are identified as such, with section numbers for relevant passages in the *CMS* given in parentheses, preceded by the number of the edition. For example, *CMS* 15 (17.288) refers to the 288th section of Chapter 17 in the fifteenth edition of the *Chicago Manual of Style*, a section that shows how to cite source material taken from the United States Constitution.

The Importance of Consistency

The most important rule regarding documentation of your work is to *be consistent*. Sloppy referencing undermines your reader's trust and does a disservice to the writers whose work you are incorporating into your own argument. And from a purely practical standpoint, inconsistent referencing can severely damage your grade.

Using the Style Manual

Read through the guidelines in the following pages before trying to use them to structure your notes. Unpracticed student researchers tend to ignore this section of the style manual until the moment the first note has to be worked out, and then they skim through the examples looking for the one that perfectly corresponds to the immediate case in hand. But most style manuals do not include every possible documentation model, so the writer must piece together a coherent reference out of elements from several examples. Reading through all the examples before using them gives you a feel for the placement of information in citations for different kinds of sources—such as magazine articles, book chapters, government documents, and electronic texts—as well as for how the referencing system works in general.

In the author-date system of citation, a note is placed in parentheses within the text, following the passage where the source material appears. In order not to distract the reader from the argument, the reference is as brief as possible, containing just enough information to refer the reader to the full citation in the reference list following the text. Usually the minimum information necessary is the author's last name, the date of the publication of the source, and if you are referring to a specific passage instead of the entire work, the page number(s) of the passage you are using. As indicated by the models below, this information can be given in a number of ways.

Models of full citations that correspond to these parenthetical text references are given in the subsection that begins on page 66. A sample reference list appears on page 73.

The Author-Date System: Citations

Author, Date, and Page in Parentheses

> Several critics found the senator's remarks to be, in the words of one, "hopelessly off the mark and dangerously incendiary" (Northrup 2006, 28).

Note that, when it appears at the end of a sentence, the parenthetical reference is placed inside the period.

Page and Chapter in Notes

A text citation may refer to an entire article, in which case you need not include page numbers, since they are given in the reference list at the end of the paper. However, you will sometimes need to cite specific page and chapter numbers, which follow the date, and are preceded by a comma and, in the case of a chapter, the abbreviation *chap.* Note that you do not use the abbreviation *p.* or *pp.* when referring to page numbers.

Page Numbers

> Randalson (2004, 84–86) provides a brief but coherent description of the bill's evolution.

Chapter Numbers

> Collins (2006, chaps. 9, 10) discusses at length the structure of the Roman senate.

Author and Date in Text

The following example focuses the reader's attention on Northrup's article:

For a highly critical review of the senator's performance, see Northrup 2006 (28).

Author in the Text, Date and Page in Parentheses

Here the emphasis is on the author, for only Northrup's name is within the grammar of the sentence:

Northrup (2006, 28) called the senator's remarks "hopelessly off the mark and dangerously incendiary."

Source with Two Authors

The administration's efforts at reforming the education system are drawing more praise than condemnation (Younger and Petty 2005).

Notice that the names are not necessarily arranged alphabetically. Use the order that the authors themselves sanctioned on the title page of the book or article.

Source with Three Authors

Most of the farmers in the region support the cooperative's new pricing plan (Moore, Macrory, and Traylor 2004, 132).

Source with Four or More Authors

Place the Latin phrase *et al.*, meaning "and others," after the name of the first author. Note that the phrase appears in roman type, not italics, and is followed by a period:

According to Herring et al. (2004, 42), five builders backed out of the project due to doubts about the local economy.

More Than One Source

Note that the references are arranged alphabetically:

Several commentators have supported the council's decision to expand the ruling (Barrere 2004; Grady 2004; Payne 2004).

Two Authors with the Same Last Name

Use a first initial to differentiate two authors with the same last name.

Research suggests that few taxpayers will appreciate the new budget cuts (B. Grady 2005; L. Grady 2004).

Two Works by the Same Author

If two references by the same author appear in the same note, place a comma between the publication dates:

George (2005, 2004) argues for sweeping tax reform on the national level.

If the two works were published in the same year, differentiate them by adding lowercase letters to the publication dates. Be sure to add the letters to the reference list, too:

> The commission's last five annual reports pointed out the same weaknesses in the structure of the city government (Estrada 2004a, 2004b).

Reprints

It is sometimes significant to note the date when an important text was first published, even if you are using a reprint of that work. In this case, the date of the first printing appears in brackets before the date of the reprint:

> During that period, there were three advertising campaign strategies that were deemed potentially useful to political campaigners (Adams [1960] 2004, 12).

Classic Texts

You may use the author-date system to structure notes for classic texts, such as the Bible, standard translations of ancient Greek works, or numbers of *The Federalist Papers*, by citing the date and page numbers of the edition you are using. Or you may refer to these texts by using the systems by which they are subdivided. Since all editions of a classic text employ the same standard subdivisions, this reference method has the advantage of allowing your reader to find the citation in any published version of the text. For example, you may cite a biblical passage by referring to the particular book, chapter, and verse, all in roman type, with the translation given after the verse number. Titles of books of the Bible should be abbreviated.

> "But the path of the just is as the shining light, that shineth more and more unto the perfect day" (Prov. 4:18 King James Version).

The Federalist Papers may be cited by their standard numbers:

> Madison addresses the problem of factions in a republic (*Federalist* 10).

Public Documents

According to the 2005 revised edition of the APSA *Style Manual*, you may cite public documents using the standard author-date technique. The *Style Manual* recommends consulting the fourteenth edition of *CMS* (16.148-98) and Chapter 12 of the latest edition of Kate L. Turabian's *Manual for Writers of Term Papers, Theses, and Dissertations* (Univ. of Chicago Press, 2004) for more detailed information. While the 2005 APSA *Style Manual* provides models of reference list entries for a few types of government documents, neither it nor the fifteenth edition of *CMS* (2003) offers corresponding examples of parenthetical text citations. The following models are based, therefore, on information taken from the APSA *Style Manual* and from Chapters 15 and 16 of the fourteenth edition of *CMS* (1993).

Congressional Journals.   Parenthetical text references to either the *Senate Journal* or the *House Journal* start with the journal title in place of the author, the session year, and, if applicable, the page:

> Senator Jones endorsed the proposal as reworded by Senator Edward's committee (*U.S. Senate Journal* 2006, 24).

Congressional Debates.   Congressional debates are printed in the daily issues of the *Congressional Record,* which are bound biweekly and then collected and bound at the end of the session. Whenever possible, you should consult the bound yearly collection instead of the biweekly compilations. Your parenthetical reference should begin with the title *Congressional Record* (or *Cong. Rec.*) in place of the author's name and include the year of the congressional session, the volume and part of the *Congressional Record,* and finally the page:

> Rep. Valentine and Rep. Beechnut addressed the question of funding for secondary education (*Cong. Rec.* 1930, 72, pt. 8: 9012).

Congressional Reports and Documents.   References to these reports and documents, which are numbered sequentially in one- or two-year periods, include the name of the body generating the material, the year, and the page:

> Rep. Slavin promised from the floor to answer the charges against him within the next week (U.S. Congress. House 2006, 12–13).

NOTE. You may omit the *U.S.,* if it is clear from the context that you are referring to the United States. Whichever form you use, be sure to use it consistently, in both the notes and the reference list.

Bills and Resolutions

The recent ruling prohibits consular officials from rejecting visa requests out of hand (U.S. Congress. Senate. 2005).

Statutes

Citing to the Statutes at Large

Congress stipulates that any book deposited for copyright in the Library of Congress that suffers serious damage or deterioration due to age be rebound in library cloth (*Book Preservation Act,* 2006, *Statutes*).

Citing to the United States Code

Congress stipulates that any book deposited for copyright in the Library of Congress that suffers serious damage or deterioration due to age be rebound in library cloth (*Book Preservation Act,* 2006, *U.S. Code*).

United States Constitution.   According to *CMS* 14 (15.367), references to the United States Constitution include the number of the article or amendment, the section number, and the clause, if necessary:

> The president has the power, in extraordinary circumstances, either to convene or to dismiss Congress (U.S. Constitution, art. 3, sec. 3).

It is not necessary to include the Constitution in the reference list.

Executive Department Documents.   A reference to a report, bulletin, circular, or any other type of material issued by the executive department starts with the name of the agency issuing the document, although you may use the name of the author, if known:

> Recent demographic projections suggest that city growth will continue to be lateral for several more years, as businesses flee downtown areas for the suburbs (Department of Labor 2004, 334).

Legal References

Supreme Court   As with laws, court decisions are rarely given their own parenthetical text citation and reference list entry, but are instead identified in the text. If you wish to use a formal reference, however, you may place within the parentheses the title of the case, in italics, followed by the source (for cases after 1875 this is the *United States Supreme Court Reports,* abbreviated *U.S.*), which is preceded by the volume number and followed by the page number.

> The judge ruled that Ms. Warren did have an obligation to offer assistance to the survivors of the wreck, an obligation which she failed to meet (*State of Nevada v. Goldie Warren* 324 U.S. 123).

Before 1875, Supreme Court decisions were published under the names of official court reporters. The reference below is to William Cranch, *Reports of Cases Argued and Adjudged in the Supreme Court of the United States, 1801–1815,* 9 vols. (Washington, DC, 1804–17). The number preceding the clerk's name is the volume number; the last number is the page:

> The first case in which the Supreme Court ruled a law of Congress to be void was *Marbury v. Madison,* in 1803 (1 Cranch 137).

For most of these parenthetical references, it is possible to move some or all of the material outside the parentheses simply by incorporating it in the text:

> In 1969, in *State of Nevada v. Goldie Warren* (324 U.S. 123), the judge ruled that an observer of a traffic accident has an obligation to offer assistance to survivors.

Lower Courts   Decisions of lower federal courts are published in the *Federal Reporter.* The note should give the volume of the *Federal Reporter* (*F.*), the series, if it is other than the first (*2d,* in the model below), the page, and, in brackets, an abbreviated reference to the specific court (the example below is to the Second Circuit Court) and the year:

One ruling takes into account the bias that often exists against the defendant in certain types of personal injury lawsuits (*United States v. Sizemore*, 183 F.2d 201 [2d Cir. 1950]).

Publications of Government Commissions. According to *CMS* 14 (15.368), references to bulletins, circulars, reports, and study papers that are issued by various government commissions should include the name of the commission, the date of the document, and the page:

> This year saw a sharp reaction among large firms to the new tax law (Securities and Exchange Commission 2004, 57).

Corporate Authors. Because government documents are often credited to a corporate author with a lengthy name, you may devise an acronym or a shortened form of the name and indicate in your first reference to the source that this name will be used in later citations:

> Government statistics over the last year showed a continuing leveling of the inflation rate (*Bulletin of Labor Statistics* 2006, 1954; *hereafter BLS*).

The practice of using a shortened name in subsequent references to any corporate author, whether a public or private organization, is sanctioned in most journals, including the *American Political Science Review,* and approved in *CMS* 14 (15.252). Thus, if you refer often to the *U.N. Monthly Bulletin of Statistics*, you may, after giving the publication's full name in the first reference, use a shortened form of the title—perhaps an acronym such as *UNMBS*—in all later cites.

Publications of State and Local Governments. According to *CMS* 14 (15.377), references to state and local government documents are similar to those for the corresponding national government sources:

> In arguing for the legality of cockfighting, Senator Lynd actually suggested that the "sport" served as a deterrent to crime among the state's young people (Oklahoma Legislature 2004, 24).

CMS 14 (16.178) restricts bibliographical information concerning state laws or municipal ordinances to the running text.

Electronic Sources

Parenthetical references to electronic sources should present the same sorts of information as references to printed sources, when possible. In other words, include the author's last name, the year of publication, and the relevant page number from the source, if given. However, some types of information that appear in standard text citations, such as the author's name and relevant page numbers, are often missing in electronic sources and so cannot appear in the reference. If the author's name is missing, the parenthetical reference can include the title of the document, in quotation marks. If the online article has numbered paragraphs, you may supply numbers for paragraphs bearing the relevant passages:

> The election results that November may have been what startled Congress into taking such an action ("Effects of Landmark Elections" 2004, para. 12–14).

Interviews

According to the revised 2005 edition of the APSA *Style Manual,* unpublished interviews should be identified within the text of a sentence rather than in a parenthetical citation. Include in the sentence the name of the interviewee, the means of communication (whether by telephone, written correspondence, or a formal, face-to-face interview), the date, and, if relevant, the location. If the interview is published, however, it should be given both a text citation and an entry in the reference list at the end of the paper.

Published Interview.

In an interview last March, Simon criticized the use of private funds to build such city projects as the coliseum (Fox 2005, 58–59).

Unpublished Interview Conducted by the Writer of the Paper.   If you are citing material from an interview that you conducted, you should identify yourself as the author and give the date of the interview:

In an interview with the author on 23 April 2004, Dr. Kennedy expressed her disappointment with the new court ruling.

The Author-Date System: Reference List

In a paper using the author-date bibliographic system, the parenthetical references point the reader to the full citations in the reference list. This list, which always follows the text of the paper, is arranged alphabetically according to the first element in each citation. Usually this element is the last name of the author or editor, but in the absence of such information, the citation is alphabetized according to the title of the work, which is then the first element in the citation.

The bibliography is double-spaced throughout, even between entries. As with most alphabetically arranged bibliographies, there is a kind of reverse indentation system called a "hanging indent": after the first line of a citation, all subsequent lines are indented five spaces.

Capitalization

The APSA *Style Manual* uses standard, or "headline style," capitalization rules for titles in the bibliographical citations. In this style, all first and last words in a title, and all other words except articles (*a, an, the*), coordinating words (*and, but, or, for, nor*), and all prepositions, are capitalized.

Books

One Author

Northrup, Alan K. 2004. *Living High Off the Hog: Recent Pork Barrel Legislation in the Senate.* Cleveland: Johnstown.

First comes the author's name, inverted, then the date of publication, followed by the title of the book, the place of publication, and the name of the publishing house. For place of publication, do not identify the state unless the city is not well known. In that case, use postal abbreviations to denote the state (*OK, AR*).

Periods are used to divide most of the elements in the citation, although a colon is used between the place of publication and publisher. Custom dictates that the main title and subtitle be separated by a colon, even though a colon may not appear in the title as printed on the title page of the book.

Two Authors. The name of only the first author is reversed, since it is the one by which the citation is alphabetized:

Spence, Michelle, and Kelly Rudd. 2005. *Education and the Law.* Boston: Tildale.

Three Authors

Moore, J. B., Jeannine Macrory, and Natasha Traylor. 2004. *Down on the Farm: Renovating the Farm Loan.* Norman: Univ. of Oklahoma Press.

According to *CMS* 15 (17.104), you may abbreviate the word *University* if it appears in the name of the press.

Four or More Authors

Herring, Ralph, et al. 2004. *Funding City Projects.* Atlanta: Jessup Institute for Policy Development.

Editor, Compiler, or Translator As Author. When no author is listed on the title page, *CMS* 15 (17.41) calls for you to begin the citation with the name of the editor, compiler, or translator, followed by the appropriate phrase—*ed., comp.,* or *trans.:*

Trakas, Dylan, comp. 2004. *Making the Road-Ways Safe; Essays on Highway Preservation and Funding.* El Paso: Del Norte Press.

Editor, Compiler, or Translator with Author. Place the name of the editor, compiler, or translator after the title, prefaced by the appropriate phrase—*Ed., Comp.,* or *Trans.:*

Pound, Ezra. 1953. *Literary Essays.* Ed. T. S. Eliot. New York: New Directions.

Stomper, Jean. 1973. *Grapes and Rain.* Trans. and ed. John Picard. New York: Baldock.

Two or More Works by the Same Author. The revised 2005 edition of the APSA *Style Manual* prohibits the replacement of an author's name in entries after the first by a three-em dash. Instead all entries by the same author must bear his or her name, and they must be arranged chronologically by publication date rather than alphabetically by title:

Russell, Henry. 1978. *Famous Last Words: Notable Supreme Court Cases of the Last Five Years.* New Orleans: Liberty Publications.

Russell, Henry, ed. 1988. *Court Battles to Remember.* Denver: Axel & Myers.

Chapter in a Multiauthor Collection

Gray, Alexa North. 2005. "Foreign Policy and the Foreign Press." In *Current Media Issues,* ed. Barbara Bonnard. New York: Boulanger.

The parenthetical text reference may include the page reference:

(Gray 2005, 191)

If the author and the editor are the same person, you must repeat the name:

Farmer, Susan A. 2004. "Tax Shelters in the New Dispensation: How to Save
   Your Income." In *Making Ends Meet: Strategies for the Nineties,* ed. Susan A.
   Farmer. Nashville: Burkette and Hyde.

Author of a Foreword or Introduction.   There is no need, according to
CMS 15 (17.46, 17.74–75), to cite the author of a foreword or introduction in
your bibliography, unless you have used material from that author's contribution
to the volume. In that case, the bibliography entry is listed under the name of the
author of the foreword or introduction. Place the name of the author of the work
itself after the title of the work:

Farris, Carla. 2004. Foreword to *Marital Stress and the Professoriat: A Case Study,*
   by Basil Givan. New York: Galapagos.

The parenthetical text reference cites the name of the author of the foreword or introduction, not the author of the book:

(Farris 2004)

Subsequent Editions.   If you are using an edition of a book other than the
first, you must cite the number of the edition or the status, such as *Rev. ed.* for
Revised edition, if there is no edition number:

Hales, Sarah. 2004. *The Coming Water Wars.* 2d ed. Pittsburgh: Blue Skies.

Multivolume Work.   If you are citing a multivolume work in its entirety, use
the following format:

Graybosch, Charles. 1988–89. *The Rise of the Unions.* 3 vols. New York:
   Starkfield.

If you are citing only one of the volumes in a multivolume work, use the
following format:

Ronsard, Madeleine. 2005. *Monopolies.* Vol. 2 of *A History of Capitalism.*
   Ed. Joseph M. Sayles. Boston: Renfrow.

Reprints

Adams, Sterling R. [1964] 1988. *How to Win an Election: Promotional Campaign Strategies.* New York: Starkfield.

Modern Editions of Classics.   If the original year of publication is known,
include it, in brackets, before the publication date for the edition used:

Burke, Edmond. [1790] 1987. *Reflections on the Revolution in France.* Ed.
   J. G. A. Pocock. Indianapolis: Hackett.

Remember, if the classic text is divided into short, numbered sections (such
as the chapter and verse divisions of the Bible), you do not need to include the
work in your bibliography unless you wish to specify a particular edition.

Periodicals

Journal Articles.   Journals are periodicals, usually published either monthly or quarterly, that specialize in serious scholarly articles in a particular field. The revised 2005 edition of the APSA *Style Manual* stipulates that a reference for a journal article must include either the month, the season, or the issue number (in that order of preference), placed just after the volume number.

> Hunzecker, Joan. 2004. "Teaching the Toadies: Cronyism in Municipal Politics." *Review of Local Politics* 4 (June): 250–62.

Note that the name of the journal, which is italicized, is followed without punctuation by the volume number. A colon separates the name of the month, in parentheses, from the inclusive page numbers. Do not use *p.* or *pp.* to introduce the page numbers.

Magazine Articles.   Magazines, which are usually published weekly, bimonthly, or monthly, appeal to the popular audience and generally have a wider circulation than journals. *Newsweek* and *Scientific American* are examples of magazines.

Monthly Magazine   The name of the magazine is separated from the month of publication by a comma:

> Stapleton, Bonnie. 1981. "How It Was: On the Campaign Trail with Ike." *Lifetime Magazine,* April, 16–21.

Weekly or Bimonthly Magazine   The day of the issue's publication appears before the month:

> Bruck, Connie. 2006. "The World of Business: A Mogul's Farewell." *The New Californian,* 18 October.

Newspaper Articles.   While the revised 2005 edition of the APSA *Style Manual* does not discuss reference list entries for newspaper articles, *CMS* 15 (15.234–42, 16.117–18) deals with the topic in some detail. Here are two typical models:

> *New York Times.* 2006. Editorial, 10 August.

> Fine, Austin. 2005. "Hoag on Trial." *Carrollton (Texas) Tribune,* 24 November.

Note that *The* is omitted from the newspaper's title. If the name of the city in which an American newspaper is published does not appear in the paper's title, it should be appended, in italics. If the city is not well known, the name of the state is added, in italics, in parentheses, as in the second model above.

Public Documents

Congressional Journals.   References to either the *Senate Journal* or the *House Journal* begin with the journal's title and include the years of the session, the number of the Congress and session, and the month and day of the entry:

> *U.S. Senate Journal.* 2006. 105th Cong., 1st sess., 10 December.

The ordinal numbers *second* and *third* may be represented as *d* (52d, 103d) or as *nd* and *rd,* respectively.

Congressional Debates

Congressional Record. 1930. 72st Cong., 2d sess., vol. 72, pt. 8.

Congressional Reports and Documents. Following the designation of Senate or House, include as many of the following items as possible, in this order: committee title, year, title of report or document, Congress, session, and report or document number or committee print number.

> U.S. Congress. House. Committee on the Budget. 2006. *Report on Government Efficiency As Perceived by the Public.* 105th Cong., 2d sess. H. Rept. 225.

Bills and Resolutions

> U.S. Congress. Senate. 2005. *Visa Formalization Act of 2005.* 105th Cong. 1st sess. S.R. 1437.

The abbreviation *S.R.* in the model above stands for *Senate Resolutions,* and the number following is the bill or resolution number. For references to House bills, the abbreviation is *H.R.*

Statutes

Citing to the Statutes at Large

> Book Preservation Act. 2006. *Statutes at Large.* Vol. 82, sec. 6, p. 184.

Citing to the United States Code

> Book Preservation Act. 2006. *U.S. Code.* Vol. 38, sec. 1562, p. 265.

United States Constitution. While the revised 2005 edition of the APSA *Style Manual* does not discuss references for the U. S. Constitution, *CMS* 14 (16.172) states that the Constitution is not listed in the bibliography.

Executive Department Documents. Include the name of the corporate author, the year, title, city, and publisher.

> Department of Labor. 2004. *Report on Urban Growth Potential Projections.* Washington, DC: GPO.

The abbreviation for the publisher in the above model, *GPO,* stands for the *Government Printing Office,* which prints and distributes most government publications. According to *CMS* 15 (15.327), you may use any of the following formats to refer to the GPO:

> Washington, DC: U.S. Government Printing Office, 2005
> Washington, DC: Government Printing Office, 2005
> Washington, DC: GPO, 2005
> Washington, DC, 2005

Remember to be consistent in using the form you choose.

Legal References

Supreme Court Use the same format as for the parenthetical text citation, only add the date after the name of the case:

> *State of Nevada v. Goldie Warren.* 1969. 324 U.S. 123.

For a case prior to 1875, use the following format:

> *Marbury v. Madison.* 1803. 1 Cranch 137.

Lower Courts   Include the volume of the *Federal Reporter* (*F.*), the series, if it is other than the first (*2d,* in the model below), the page, and, in parentheses, an abbreviated reference to the specific district.

> *United States v. Sizemore.* 1950. 183 F.2d 201 (2d Cir.).

Publications of Government Commissions

> U.S. Securities and Exchange Commission. 1984. *Annual Report of the Securities and Exchange Commission for the Fiscal Year.* Washington, DC: GPO.

Publications of State and Local Governments.   Remember that references for state and local government publications are modeled on those for corresponding national government documents:

> Oklahoma Legislature. 2006. Joint Committee on Public Recreation. *Final Report to the Legislature, 2006, Regular Session, on Youth Activities.* Oklahoma City.

Electronic Sources

If a source is available in both print and electronic forms, it is preferable to use the print form, which is probably more readily available to readers than the electronic form. But if you have used the electronic version and it is different from the print version, the general practice is to make your reference to the electronic source as similar as possible to that for the print version, adding the full retrieval path (the electronic address) and the date of your last access of the material.

Electronic Book.   Begin with the author's name, reversed, followed if possible by date of publication, then the title of the work, the retrieval path, and the date of your last access to the work, in parentheses.

> Amshiral, Sretas. 2004. *Aviation in the Far East.* http://www.flight_easthist.org (January 3, 2005).

Chapter in an Electronic Book

> Burris, Akasha. 2004. "Experiments in Transubstantiation." *Surviving Global Disaster.* http://www.meekah/exit/paleoearth.html (March 5, 2005).

Note that you may continue a lengthy URL on the next line of the reference. Do not add a hyphen at the end of the first line.

Electronic Journals.   Include all of the following information that you can find, in this order: name of author, reversed; year of publication; title of article, in quotation marks; title of journal, in italics; any further publication information, such as volume number, day or month; full retrieval path; and date of your last access, in parentheses:

> Zoheret, Jeanie. 2003. "The Politics of Social Deprivation." *B & N Digest* 3 (February). http://postmodern/tsu/b&n.edu (December 5, 2004).

Material from a World Wide Web (WWW) Site.   The author's name (reversed) and year of publication are followed by the title of the article, in quotation marks; the title, if applicable, of the complete work or Web page, in italics; the full Web address (URL); and, finally, the date on which you last accessed the page, in parentheses:

> Squires, Lawrence. 2004. "A Virtual Tour of the White House, circa 1900." *National Landmarks: Then and Now.* http://www.natlandmk.com/hist (August 21, 2004).

E-Mail Material.   The revised 2005 edition of the APSA *Style Manual* suggests that e-mail, bulletin board, and electronic discussion group messages be cited as personal communication in the text and left out of the reference list.

Interviews

Published Interviews

Untitled Interview in a Book

> Jorgenson, Mary. 2004. Interview by Alan McAskill. In *Hospice Pioneers.* Ed. Alan McAskill, 62–86. Richmond: Dynasty Press.

Titled Interview in a Periodical

> Simon, John. 2004. "Picking the Patrons Apart: An Interview with John Simon." By Selena Fox. *Media Week,* March 14, 40–46.

Interview on Television

> Snopes, Edward. 2004. Interview by Klint Gordon. *Oklahoma Politicians.* WKY Television, 4 June.

Unpublished Interview.   According to the revised 2005 edition of the APSA *Style Manual,* unpublished interviews should be identified within the text of a sentence rather than in a parenthetical citation and left out of the reference list.

Unpublished Sources

Theses and Dissertations.   If the work has a sewn or glued binding, place the title in italics, like a book; otherwise designate the title by quotation marks:

> Hochenauer, Art. 2005. *Populism and the Free Soil Movement.* Ph.D. diss. University of Virginia.
>
> Sharpe, Ellspeth Stanley. 2003. "Black Women in Politics: A Troubled History." Master's thesis. Oregon State University.

Paper Presented at a Meeting

> Zelazny, Kim, and Ed Gilmore. 2005. "Art for Art's Sake: Funding the NEA in the Twenty-First Century." Presented at the Annual Meeting of the Conference of Metropolitan Arts Councils, San Francisco.

Manuscript in the Author's Possession

Borges, Rita V. 1969. "Mexican-American Border Conflicts, 1915–1970." University of Texas at El Paso. Photocopy.

The entry includes the institution with which the author is affiliated and ends with a description of the format of the work (typescript, photocopy, etc.).

Sample Bibliography: APSA Author-Date System

NOTE. Most of the sources used as models in this chapter are not references to actual publications.

Ariès, Philippe. 1962. <u>Centuries of Childhood: A Social History</u> of <u>Family Life</u>. Trans. Robert Baldock. New York: Knopf.

Cesbron, Henry. 1909. <u>Histoire critique de l'hystérie</u>. Paris: Asselin et Houzeau.

Farmer, Susan A. 2004. "Tax Shelters in the New Dispensation: How to Save Your Income." In <u>Making Ends Meet: Strategies for the Nineties</u>, ed. Susan A. Farmer. Nashville: Burkette and Hyde.

Herring, Ralph, et al. 2004. <u>Funding City Projects</u>. Atlanta: Jessup Institute for Policy Development.

Hunzecker, Joan. 2004. "Teaching the Toadies: Cronyism in Municipal Politics." <u>Review of Local Politics</u> 4:250–62.

Moore, J. B., Jeannine Macrory, and Natasha Traylor. 2004. <u>Down on the Farm: Renovating the Farm Loan</u>. Norman: Univ. of Oklahoma Press.

Northrup, Alan K. 2004. <u>Living High Off the Hog: Recent Pork Barrel Legislation in the Senate</u>. Cleveland: Johnstown.

Skylock, Browning. 1991. "'Fifty-Four Forty or Fight!': Sloganeering in Early America." <u>American History Digest</u> 28(3): 25–34.

Squires, Lawrence. 2006. "A Virtual Tour of the White House, circa 1900." *National Landmarks: Then and Now.* http://www.natlandmk.com/hist (21 August 2004).

Stapleton, Bonnie. 1981. "How It Was: On the Campaign Trail with Ike." <u>Lifetime Magazine</u>, April.

U.S. Securities and Exchange Commission. 1984. <u>Annual Report of the Securities and Exchange Commission for the Fiscal Year</u>. Washington, 2005.

4.2   AVOIDING PLAGIARISM

You want to use your source material as effectively as possible. This will sometimes mean that you should quote from a source directly, whereas at other times you will want to express such information in your own words. At all times, you should work to integrate the source material skillfully into the flow of your written argument.

When to Quote

You should quote directly from a source when the original language is distinctive enough to enhance your argument, or when rewording the passage would lessen its impact. In the interest of fairness, you should also quote a passage to which you will take exception. Rarely, however, should you quote a source at great length (longer than two or three paragraphs). Nor should your paper, or any substantial section of it, be merely a string of quoted passages. The more language you take from the writings of others, the more the quotations will disrupt the rhetorical flow of your own words. Too much quoting creates a choppy patchwork of varying styles and borrowed purposes in which your sense of your own control over your material is lost.

Quotations in Relation to Your Writing

When you do use a quotation, make sure that you insert it skillfully. According to the APSA *Style Manual*, quotations of four lines or fewer should be integrated into your text and set off with quotation marks:

> "In the last analysis," Alice Thornton argued in 2006, "we cannot afford not to embark on a radical program of fiscal reform" (12).

Quotations longer than four lines should begin on a new line and be indented five spaces from the left margin:

> Blake's outlook for the solution to the city's problem of abandoned buildings is anything but optimistic:
>
> > If the trend in demolitions due to abandonment continues, the cost of doing nothing may be too high. The three-year period from 2004 to 2004 shows an annual increase in demolitions of roughly twenty percent. Such an upward trend for a sustained period of time would eventually place a disastrous hardship on the city's resources. And yet the city council seems bent on following the tactic of inaction.(2004, 8)

Acknowledge Quotations Carefully

Failing to signal the presence of a quotation skillfully can lead to confusion or choppiness:

> The U.S. Secretary of Labor believes that worker retraining programs have failed because of a lack of trust within the American business culture.

"The American business community does not visualize the need to invest in its workers" (Winn 2004, 11).

The first sentence in the above passage seems to suggest that the quote that follows comes from the Secretary of Labor. Note how this revision clarifies the attribution:

According to reporter Fred Winn, the U.S. Secretary of Labor believes that worker retraining programs have failed because of a lack of trust within the American business culture. Summarizing the secretary's view, Winn writes, "The American business community does not visualize the need to invest in its workers" (2004, 11).

The origin of each quote must be indicated within your text at the point where the quote occurs as well as in the list of works cited, which follows the text.

Quote Accurately

If your transcription of a quotation introduces careless variants of any kind, you are misrepresenting your source. Proofread your quotations very carefully, paying close attention to such surface features as spelling, capitalization, italics, and the use of numerals.

Occasionally, in order to make a quotation fit smoothly into a passage, to clarify a reference, or to delete unnecessary material, you may need to change the original wording slightly. You must, however, signal any such change to your reader. Some alterations may be noted by brackets:

"Several times in the course of his speech, the attorney general said that his stand [on gun control] remains unchanged" (McAffrey 2004, 2).

Ellipses indicate that words have been left out of a quote:

"The last time voters refused to endorse one of the senator's policies . . . was back in 1982" (Laws 2005, 143).

When you integrate quoted material with your own prose, it is unnecessary to begin the quote with ellipses:

Benton raised eyebrows with his claim that "nobody in the mayor's office knows how to tie a shoe, let alone balance a budget" (Williams 2006, 12).

Paraphrasing

Your writing has its own rhetorical attributes, its own rhythms and structural coherence. Inserting several quotations into one section of your paper can disrupt the patterns of your prose and diminish its effectiveness. Paraphrasing, or recasting source material in your own words, is one way to avoid the choppiness that can result from a series of quotations.

Remember that a paraphrase is to be written in your language; it is not a near-copy of the source writer's language. Merely changing a few words of the original does justice to no one's prose and frequently produces stilted passages. This sort of borrowing is actually a form of plagiarism. To integrate another's material into your own writing fully, use your own language.

Paraphrasing may actually increase your comprehension of source material, because in recasting a passage you will have to think very carefully about its meaning—more carefully, perhaps, than if you had merely copied it word for word.

Avoiding Plagiarism When Paraphrasing

Paraphrases require the same sort of documentation as direct quotes. The words of a paraphrase may be yours, but the idea belongs to someone else. Failure to give that person credit, in the form of references within the text and in the bibliography, may make you vulnerable to a charge of plagiarism.

Plagiarism is the use of someone else's words or ideas without proper credit. Although some plagiarism is deliberate, produced by writers who understand that they are guilty of a kind of academic thievery, much of it is unconscious, committed by writers who are not aware of the varieties of plagiarism or who are careless in recording their borrowings from sources. Plagiarism includes:

- Quoting directly without acknowledging the source
- Paraphrasing without acknowledging the source
- Constructing a paraphrase that closely resembles the original in language and syntax

One way to guard against plagiarism is to keep careful notes of when you have directly quoted source material and when you have paraphrased—making sure that the wording of the paraphrases is yours. Be sure that all direct quotes in your final draft are properly set off from your own prose, either with quotation marks or in indented blocks.

What kind of paraphrased material must be acknowledged? Basic material that you find in several sources need not be documented by a reference. For example, it is unnecessary to cite a source for the information that Franklin Delano Roosevelt was elected to a fourth term as president of the United States shortly before his death, because this is a commonly known fact. However, Professor Smith's opinion, published in a recent article, that Roosevelt's winning of a fourth term hastened his death is not a fact, but a theory based on Smith's research and defended by her. If you wish to use Smith's opinion in a paraphrase, you need to credit her, as you should all judgments and claims from another source. Any information that is not widely known, whether factual or open to dispute, should be documented. This includes statistics, graphs, tables, and charts taken from sources other than your own primary research.

◆ CHAPTER 5 ◆
Organizing the Research Process

5.1 GAINING CONTROL OF THE RESEARCH PROCESS

The research paper is where all your skills as an interpreter of details, an organizer of facts and theories, and a writer of clear prose come together. Building logical arguments on the twin bases of fact and hypothesis is the way things are done in political science, and the most successful political scientists are those who master the art of research.

Students new to the writing of research papers sometimes find themselves intimidated by the job ahead of them. After all, the research paper adds what seems to be an extra set of complexities to the writing process. As any other expository or persuasive paper does, a research paper must present an original thesis using a carefully organized and logical argument. But a research paper also investigates a topic that is outside the writer's own experience. This means that writers must locate and evaluate information that is new, in effect educating themselves as they explore their topics. A beginning researcher sometimes feels overwhelmed by the basic requirements of the assignment or by the authority of the source material being investigated.

As you begin a research project, it may be difficult to establish a sense of control over the different tasks you are undertaking. You may have little notion of where to search for a thesis or even for the most helpful information. If you do not carefully monitor your own work habits, you may find yourself unwittingly abdicating responsibility for the paper's argument by borrowing it wholesale from one or more of your sources.

Who is in control of your paper? The answer must be you—not the instructor who assigned you the paper, and certainly not the published writers and interviewees whose opinions you solicit. If all your paper does is paste together the opinions of others, it has little use. It is up to you to synthesize an original idea from a judicious evaluation of your source material. At the beginning of your research project, you will of course be unsure about many elements of your paper. For example, you will probably not yet have a definitive thesis sentence or even much understanding of the shape of your argument. But you can establish a measure of control over the process you will go through to complete the paper. And, if you work regularly and systematically, keeping yourself open to new ideas as they present themselves, your sense of control will grow. Here are some suggestions to help you establish and maintain control of your paper:

1. *Understand your assignment.* It is possible for a research assignment to go badly simply because the writer did not read the assignment carefully. Considering how much time and effort you are about to put into your project, it is a very good idea to make sure you have a clear understanding of what your instructor wants you to do. Be sure to ask your instructor about any aspect of the assignment that is unclear to you—but only after you have read it carefully. Recopying the assignment in your own handwriting is a good way to start, even though your instructor may have already given it to you in writing. Before you dive into the project, make sure that you have considered the questions listed below.

2. *What is your topic?* The assignment may give you a great deal of specific information about your topic, or you may be allowed considerable freedom in establishing one for yourself. In a government class in which you are studying issues affecting American foreign policy, your professor might give you a very specific assignment—a paper, for example, examining the difficulties of establishing a viable foreign policy in the wake of the collapse of international communism—or she may allow you to choose for yourself the issue that your paper will address. You need to understand the terms, as set up in the assignment, by which you will design your project.

3. *What is your purpose?* Whatever the degree of latitude you are given in the matter of your topic, pay close attention to the way your instructor has phrased the assignment. Is your primary job to *describe* a current political situation or to *take a stand* on it? Are you to *compare* political systems, and if so, to what end? Are you to *classify, persuade, survey, analyze?* To determine the purpose of the project, look for such descriptive terms in the assignment.

4. *Who is your audience?* Your own orientation to the paper is profoundly affected by your conception of the audience for which you are writing. Granted, your main reader is your instructor, but who else would be interested in your paper? Are you writing for the voters of a community? a governor? a city council? A paper that describes the proposed renovation of city buildings may justifiably contain much more technical jargon for an audience of contractors than for a council of local business and civic leaders.

5. *What kind of research are you doing?* You will be doing one if not both of the following kinds of research:

• *Primary research,* which requires you to discover information firsthand, often by conducting interviews, surveys, or polls. In primary research, you are collecting and sifting through raw data—data that have not already been interpreted by researchers—which you will then study, select, arrange, and speculate on. These raw data may be the opinions of experts or of people on the street, historical documents, the published letters of a famous politician, or material collected from other researchers. It is important to set up carefully the methods by which you collect your data. Your aim is to gather the most accurate information possible, from which sound observations may be made later, either by you or by other writers using the material you have uncovered.

   • *Secondary research,* which uses published accounts of primary materials. Whereas the primary researcher might poll a community for its opinion on the outcome of a recent bond election, the secondary researcher will use the material from the poll to support a particular thesis. Secondary research, in other words, focuses on interpretations of raw data. Most of your college papers will be based on your use of secondary sources.

PRIMARY SOURCE	SECONDARY SOURCE
A published collection of Thurgood Marshall's letters	A journal article arguing that the volume of letters illustrates Marshall's attitude toward the media
An interview with the mayor	A character study of the mayor based on the interview
Material from a questionnaire	A paper basing its thesis on the results of the questionnaire

   6. *Keep your perspective.* Whichever type of research you perform, you must keep your results in perspective. There is no way that you, as a primary researcher, can be completely objective in your findings. It is not possible to design a questionnaire that will net you absolute truth, nor can you be sure that the opinions you gather in interviews reflect the accurate and unchanging opinions of the people you question. Likewise, if you are conducting secondary research, you must remember that the articles and journals you are reading are shaped by the aims of their writers, who are interpreting primary materials for their own ends. The farther you are removed from a primary source, the greater the possibility for distortion. Your job as a researcher is to be as accurate as possible, which means keeping in view the limitations of your methods and their ends.

5.2   EFFECTIVE RESEARCH METHODS

   In any research project there will be moments of confusion, but you can prevent this confusion from overwhelming you by establishing an effective research procedure. You need to design a schedule that is as systematic as possible, yet flexible enough so that you do not feel trapped by it. By always showing you what to do next, a schedule will help keep you from running into dead ends.

At the same time, the schedule helps you retain the focus necessary to spot new ideas and new strategies as you work.

Give Yourself Plenty of Time

You may feel like delaying your research for many reasons: unfamiliarity with the library, the press of other tasks, a deadline that seems comfortably far away. But do not allow such factors to deter you. Research takes time. Working in a library seems to speed up the clock, so that the hour you expected it would take you to find a certain source becomes two. You must allow yourself the time needed not only to find material but also to read it, assimilate it, and set it in the context of your own thoughts. If you delay starting, you may well find yourself distracted by the deadline, having to keep an eye on the clock while trying to make sense of a writer's complicated argument.

The following schedule lists the steps of a research project in the order in which they are generally accomplished. Remember that each step is dependent on the others and that it is quite possible to revise earlier decisions in the light of later discoveries. After some background reading, for example, your notion of the paper's purpose may change, a fact that may in turn alter other steps. One of the strengths of a good schedule is its flexibility. Note that this schedule lists tasks for both primary and secondary research; you should use only those steps that are relevant to your project.

Do Background Reading

Whether you are doing primary or secondary research, you need to know what kinds of work have already been done in your field. A good way to start is by consulting general reference works, though you do not want to overdo it (see below). Chapters 6 and 7 list specialized reference works on topics of interest to political scientists on the Internet. You might find help in such sources even for specific local problems, such as how to restructure a city council or finance an antidrug campaign in area schools.

WARNING. Be very careful not to rely too heavily on material in general encyclopedias, such as the *Encyclopaedia Britannica* or *Collier's Encyclopedia*. You may wish to consult one for an overview of a topic with which you are unfamiliar, but students new to research are often tempted to import large sections, if not entire articles, from such volumes, and this practice is not good scholarship. One major reason your instructor has assigned a research paper is to let you experience the kinds of books and journals in which the discourse of political science is conducted. Encyclopedias are good places for instant introductions to subjects; some even include bibliographies of reference works at the ends of their articles. But to write a useful paper you will need much more detailed information about your subject. Once you have learned what you can from a general encyclopedia, move on to other sources.

A primary rule of source hunting is to *use your imagination*. Determine what topics relevant to your study might be covered in general reference works. If, for example, you are looking for introductory readings to help you with a research paper on antidrug campaign financing, you might look into such specialized reference tools as the *Encyclopedia of Social Work*. Remember to check articles in such works for lists of references to specialized books and essays.

Narrow Your Topic and Establish a Working Thesis

Before exploring outside sources, you should find out what you already know or think about your topic, a job that can be accomplished well only in writing. You might wish to investigate your own attitude toward your topic by using one or more of the prewriting strategies described in Chapter 1. You might also be surprised by what you know—or don't know—about the subject. This kind of self-questioning can help you discover a profitable direction for your research.

For a research paper in a course in American government, Charlotte Goble was given the topic category of grassroots attempts to legislate morality in American society. She chose the specific topic of textbook censorship. Here is the path she took as she looked for ways to limit the topic effectively and find a thesis:

GENERAL TOPIC	Textbook censorship
POTENTIAL TOPICS	How a local censorship campaign gets started
	Funding censorship campaigns
	Reasons behind textbook censorship
	Results of censorship campaigns
WORKING THESIS	It is disconcertingly easy in our part of the state to launch a textbook censorship campaign.

Specific methods for discovering a thesis are discussed in Chapter 1. It is unlikely that you will come up with a satisfactory thesis at the beginning of your project. You need a way to guide yourself through the early stages of research as you work toward discovering a main idea that is both useful and manageable. Having in mind a *working thesis*—a preliminary statement of your purpose—can help you select the material that is of greatest interest to you as you examine potential sources. The working thesis will probably evolve as your research progresses, and you should be ready to accept such change. You must not fix on a thesis too early in the process, or you may miss opportunities to refine it.

Develop a Working Bibliography

As you begin your research, you will look for published sources—essays, books, interviews with experts—that may help you. This list of potentially useful sources is your *working bibliography*. There are many ways to develop this bibliography. The cataloging system in your library will give you sources, as will published bibliographies in your field. (Some of these bibliographies are listed below.) The general references in which you did your background reading may also list such works, and each specialized book or essay you find will have a bibliography that its writer used, which may be helpful to you.

It is from your working bibliography that you will select the items for the bibliography that will appear in the final draft of your paper. Early in your research you will not know which of the sources will help you and which will not, but it is important to keep an accurate description of each entry in your working bibliography so that you will be able to tell clearly which items you have investigated and which you will need to consult again. Establishing the working bibliography also allows you to practice using the bibliographical format you are required to follow in your final draft. As you make your list of potential sources, be sure to include all the information about each one, in the proper format, using the proper punctuation. (Chapter 4 describes in detail the bibliographical formats most often required for political science papers.)

Write for Needed Information

In the course of your research you may need to consult a source that is not immediately available to you. Working on the antidrug campaign paper, for example, you might find that a packet of potentially useful information may be obtained from a government agency or public interest group in Washington, DC. Or you may discover that a needed book is not owned by your university library or by any other local library, or that a successful antidrug program has been implemented in the school system of a city of comparable size in another state. In such situations, it may be tempting to disregard potential sources because of the difficulty of consulting them. If you ignore this material, however, you are not doing your job.

It is vital that you take steps to acquire the needed data. In the first case above, you can simply write to the Washington, DC, agency or interest group; in the second, you may use your library's interlibrary loan procedure to obtain the book; in the third, you can track down the council that manages the antidrug campaign by mail, phone, or Internet, and ask for information. Remember that many businesses and government agencies want to share their information with interested citizens; some have employees or entire departments whose job is to facilitate communication with the public. Be as specific as possible when asking for such information. It is a good idea to outline your own project briefly—in no more than a few sentences—to help the respondent determine the types of information that will be useful to you.

Never let the immediate unavailability of a source stop you from trying to consult it. And be sure to begin the job of locating and acquiring such long-distance material as soon as possible, to allow for the various delays that often occur.

Evaluate Written Sources

Fewer research experiences are more frustrating than trying to recall information found in a source that you can no longer identify. You must establish an efficient method of examining and evaluating the sources in your working bibliography. Suggestions for compiling an accurate record of your written sources are described below.

Determine Quickly the Potential Usefulness of a Source

For books, you can read the front material (the introduction, foreword, and preface), looking for the author's thesis; you can also examine chapter headings, dust jackets, and indexes. A journal article should announce its intention in its introduction, which in most cases will be a page or less in length. This sort of preliminary examination should tell you whether a more intensive examination is worthwhile. *Whatever you decide about the source, photocopy its title page,* making sure to include all important publication information (including title, date, author, volume number, and page numbers). Write on the photocopied page any necessary information that is not printed there. Without such a record, later in your research you might forget that you have consulted a particular text and find yourself repeating your work.

When you have determined that a potential source is worth closer inspection, explore it carefully. If it is a book, determine whether you should invest the time needed to read it in its entirety. Whatever the source, make sure you understand not only its overall thesis, but also each part of the argument that the writer sets up to illustrate or prove the thesis. You need to get a feel for the writer's argument—how the subtopics form (or do not form) a logical defense of the main point. What do you think of the writer's logic and the examples used? You may need more than one reading to arrive at an accurate appraisal.

As you read, try to get a feel for the larger argument in which the source takes its place. Its references to the works of other writers will show you where to look for additional material and indicate the general shape of scholarly opinion concerning your subject. If you can see the source you are reading as only one element of an ongoing dialogue, instead of the last word on the subject, then you can place its argument in perspective.

Use Photocopies

Periodicals and most reference works cannot be checked out of the library. Before the widespread availability of photocopy machines, students could use these materials only in the library, jotting down information on note cards. Although there are advantages to using the note card method (see below), photocopying saves you time in the library and allows you to take the original information home, where you can decide how to use it at your convenience.

If you do decide to copy source material, you should do the following:

- Be sure to follow all copyright laws.
- Have the exact change for the photocopy machines. Do not trust the change machines at the library. They are sometimes battle-scarred and cantankerous.
- Record all necessary bibliographical information on the photocopy. If you forget to do this, you might find yourself having to make an extra trip to the library just to get a date of publication or page numbers.

Remember that photocopying a source is not the same as examining it. You will still have to spend time going over the material, assimilating it to use it accurately. It is not enough merely to have the information close at hand or even to have read it once or twice. You must understand it thoroughly. Be sure to give yourself time for this kind of evaluation.

The Note Card—A Thing of the Past?   In many ways, note cards are an old-fashioned method of recording source material, and for unpracticed researchers, they may seem unwieldy and unnecessary, because the information jotted on them—one fact per card—will eventually have to be transmitted again, in the research paper. However, before you decide to abolish the note card system once and for all, consider its advantages:

1. Using note cards is a way of forcing yourself to think productively as you read. In translating the language of the source into the language of your notes, you are assimilating the material more completely than you would by merely reading it.

2. Note cards give you a handy way to arrange and rearrange your facts, looking for the best possible organization for your paper. Not even a computer gives you the flexibility of a pack of cards as you try to order your paper.

Determine Whether Interviews or Surveys Are Needed

If your project calls for primary research, you may need to use a questionnaire to interview experts on your topic or to conduct a survey of opinions among a select group. Be sure to prepare yourself as thoroughly as possible for any primary research. Here are some tips:

Conducting an Interview

Establish a purpose for each interview, bearing in mind the requirements of your working thesis. In what ways might your interview benefit your paper? Write down your description of the interview's purpose. Estimate its length, and inform your subject. Arrive for your interview on time and dressed appropriately. Be courteous.

Before the interview, learn as much as possible about your topic by researching published sources. Use this research to design your questions. If possible, learn something about the backgrounds of the people you interview. This knowledge may help you establish rapport with your subjects and will also help you tailor your questions. Take with you to the interview a list of prepared questions. However, be ready during the interview to depart from your list in order to follow any potentially useful direction that the questioning may take.

Take notes. Make sure you have extra pens. Do not use a tape recorder, because it will inhibit most interviewees. If you must use tape, *ask for permission from your subject* before beginning the interview. Follow up your interview with a thank-you letter and, if feasible, a copy of the paper in which the interview is used.

Designing and Conducting a Survey

If your research requires a survey, see Chapter 14 for instructions on designing and conducting surveys, polls, and questionnaires.

Draft a Thesis and Outline

No matter how thoroughly you may hunt for data or how fast you read, you will not be able to find and assimilate every source pertaining to your subject, especially if it is popular or controversial, and you should not unduly prolong your research. You must bring this phase of the project to an end—with the option of resuming it if the need arises—and begin to shape both the material you have gathered and your thoughts about it into a paper. During the research phase of your project, you have been thinking about your working thesis, testing it against the material you have discovered and considering ways to improve it. Eventually, you must formulate a thesis that sets out an interesting and useful task, one that can be satisfactorily managed within the limits of your assignment and that effectively employs much, if not all, of the material you have gathered.

Once you have formulated your thesis, it is a good idea to make an outline of the paper. In helping you to determine a structure for your writing, the outline is also testing the thesis, prompting you to discover the kinds of work your paper will need to complete the task set out by the main idea. Chapter 1 discusses the structural requirements of the formal and the informal outline. (If you have used note cards, you may want to start outlining by organizing your cards according to the headings you have given them and looking for logical connections among the different groups of cards. Experimenting with structure in this way may lead you to discoveries that will further improve your thesis.)

No thesis or outline is written in stone. There is still time to improve the structure or purpose of your paper even after you have begun to write your first draft or, for that matter, your final draft. Some writers actually prefer to write a first draft before outlining, and then study the draft's structure to determine what revisions need to be made. *Stay flexible,* always looking for a better connection, a sharper wording of your thesis. All the time you are writing, the testing of your ideas continues.

Write a First Draft

Despite all the preliminary work you have done on your paper, you may feel a reluctance to begin your first draft. Integrating all your material and your ideas into a smoothly flowing argument is indeed a complicated task. It may help to think of your first attempt as only a rough draft, which can be changed as necessary. Another strategy for reducing reluctance to start is to begin with the part of the draft about which you feel most confident, instead of with the introduction. You may write sections of the draft in any order, piecing the parts together later. But however you decide to start writing—**START**.

Obtain Feedback

It is not enough that you understand your argument; others have to understand it, too. If your instructor is willing to look at your rough draft, you should take advantage of the opportunity and pay careful attention to any suggestions for improvement. Other readers may also be of help, although having a friend or a relative read your draft may not be as helpful as having it read by someone who is knowledgeable in your field. In any event, be sure to evaluate any suggestions carefully. Remember, the final responsibility for the paper rests with you.

5.3 HOW TO CONDUCT A LITERATURE REVIEW

Your goal in writing a research paper is to provide an opportunity for your readers to increase their understanding of the subject you are addressing. They will want the most current and precise information available. Whether you are writing a traditional library research paper, conducting an experiment, or preparing an analysis of a policy enforced by a government agency, you must know what has already been learned in order to give your readers comprehensive and up-to-date information or to add something new to what they already know about the subject. If your topic is welfare administration in Tennessee, for example, you will want to find out precisely what national, state, and local government policies currently affect welfare administration in Tennessee, and the important details of how and why these policies came to be adopted. When you seek this information, you will be conducting a *literature review,* a thoughtful collection and analysis of available information on the topic you have selected for study. It tells you, before you begin your paper, experiment, or analysis, what is already known about the subject.

Why do you need to conduct a literature review? It would be embarrassing to spend a lot of time and effort preparing a study, only to find that the information you are seeking has already been discovered by someone else. Also, a properly conducted literature review will tell you many things about a particular subject. It will tell you the extent of current knowledge, sources of data for your research, examples of what is *not* known (which in turn generate ideas for formulating hypotheses), methods that have been previously used for research, and clear definitions of concepts relevant to your own research.

Let us consider an example. Suppose that you have decided to research the following question: "How are voter attitudes affected by negative advertising?" First, you will need to establish a clear definition of "negative advertising"; then you will need to find a way to measure attitudes of voters; and finally, you will need to use or develop a method of discerning how attitudes are affected by advertising. Using research techniques explained in this and other chapters of this manual, you will begin your research by looking for studies that address your research question or similar questions in the library, on the Internet, and through other resources. You will discover that many studies have been written on voters' attitudes and the effects of advertising on them. As you read these studies, certain patterns will appear. Some research methods will seem to have produced better results than others. Some studies will be quoted in others many times—some confirming and others refuting what previous studies have done. You will constantly be making choices as you examine these studies, reading very carefully those that are highly relevant to your purposes, and skimming those that are of only marginal interest. As you read, constantly ask yourself the following questions:

- How much is known about this subject?
- What is the best available information, and why is it better than other information?
- What research methods have been used successfully in relevant studies?
- What are the possible sources of data for further investigation of this topic?
- What important information is still not known, in spite of all previous research?
- Of the methods that have been used for research, which are the most effective for making new discoveries? Are new methods needed?
- How can the concepts being researched be more precisely defined?

You will find that this process, like the research process as a whole, is recursive: insights related to one of the above questions will spark new investigations into others, these investigations will then bring up a new set of questions, and so on.

Your instructor may request that you include a literature review as a section of the paper that you are writing. Your written literature review may be from one to several pages in length, but it should always tell the reader the following information:

1. Which previously compiled or published studies, articles, or other documents provide the best available information on the selected topic
2. What these studies conclude about the topic
3. What the apparent methodological strengths and weaknesses of these studies are
4. What remains to be discovered about the topic
5. What appear to be, according to these studies, the most effective methods for developing new information on the topic

Your literature review should consist of a written narrative that answers—not necessarily consecutively—the above questions. The success of your own research project depends in large part on the extent to which you have carefully and thoughtfully answered these questions.

◆ CHAPTER 6 ◆
Library Information Resources

You will find a vast amount of information about writing, politics, and government in your college library. There is, in fact, so much information that discovering where to start looking can be a substantial task in itself. This section lists some important guides to information about politics and government that may help you launch your research project.

6.1   REFERENCE BOOKS

Reference Books: American Government and Politics

Barone, Michael, and Grant Ujifusa. *The Almanac of American Politics*. Washington, DC: National Journal. Annual. This compendium of information on national and state governments and officeholders includes essays, organized alphabetically by state, on U.S. governors, senators, and representatives. Charts summarize yearly voting records of each official. An index is included.

Budget of the United States Government. Washington, DC: Government Printing Office. Annual. The yearly government printing of the budget organizes its discussion of federal spending by specific current issues, then details the budgets of the specific government agencies. There is an index.

Congressional Quarterly Almanac. Washington, DC: Congressional Quarterly. Annual. This overview of legislation for the year's session of Congress is organized by subject headings, for example, "Economics and Finance" and "Government/Commerce." There are three indexes: a bill number index, a roll-call vote index, and a general index.

Gimlin, Hoyt, ed. *Historic Documents*. Washington, DC: Congressional Quarterly. Annual. This series of yearly volumes publishes a selection of the current year's government documents. Chosen to reflect the editor's assessment of important events, the documents are organized chronologically, and the volumes are indexed every five years.

Graham, Judith, ed. *Current Biography Yearbook*. New York: H. W. Wilson. Annual. The essays in this series, some of them more than a page in length, sketch biographies of distinguished individuals from a variety of fields. Each entry includes a list of references. Contents are indexed by profession.

Inventory of Information Sources and Services Available to the U.S. House of Representatives. 1977. Westport, CT: Greenwood. This volume lists the tremendous number of information sources, both public and private, used by representatives. There is a general index.

Kay, Ernest. *Dictionary of International Biography.* Cambridge, MA: Melrose Press. Annual. This volume publishes brief biographical citations of individuals of interest in several fields. There is no index.

Mooney, Louis, ed. *The Annual Obituary.* Detroit: St. James Press. Annual. This series prints brief essays on notable individuals who died during the year. Each entry includes references. The volumes are indexed by profession.

Morris, Dan, and Inez Morris. 1974. *Who Was Who in American Politics.* New York: Hawthorn Books. A one-volume reference identifying approximately 4,200 national political figures either inactive in politics or deceased. Brief biographical descriptions list offices held. There is no index.

The National Cyclopedia of American Biography. New York: James T. White. Annual to 1978. This series of volumes, the first of which was issued in 1888, offers biographical essays on notable Americans, in a variety of fields, who were alive at the time of publication. An index of names is included.

Plano, Jack C., and Milton Greenburg. 1997. *The American Political Dictionary.* 10th ed. Fort Worth: Harcourt Brace Jovanovich. This dictionary offers concise definitions of more than 4,000 terms of interest in politics and political science. Important terms are given more in-depth treatment. There is an index.

Public Papers of the Presidents. Washington, DC: Government Printing Office. This government series publishes the papers and speeches of every U.S. president since Herbert Hoover, except for Franklin D. Roosevelt, whose papers were published privately. There is a separate set of volumes for each president.

Schwarzkopf, LeRoy, comp. *Government Reference Books: A Biennial Guide to U.S. Government Publications.* Englewood, CO: Libraries Unlimited. Biennial. This listing of government reference books is part of a series that began in 1968–69. The entry for each government publication includes address, publication information, and a brief description of the contents. The entries are arranged by topic.

Troshynski-Thomas, Karen, and Deborah M. Burek, eds. *Gale Directory of Publications and Broadcast Media.* Detroit: Gale Research. (Formerly the Ayer Dictionary of Publications.) Annual. Volumes 1 and 2 of each year's edition list and describe briefly periodicals published in the United States and Canada, as well as radio and television stations and media cable systems. Entries are arranged by state and town. There is also a brief tally of information for each state, giving population and total number of newspapers and television stations. Volume 3 includes several indexes, tables, and maps.

United States Code. Washington, DC: Government Printing Office. This massive, multivolume publication, updated every six to eight years, prints all of the country's laws that are currently in force. Separate volumes index the contents.

Who Was Who in America, with World Notables. 2002. 15 vols. New Providence, NJ: Marquis Who's Who. This series publishes brief biographies of national and international figures who were no longer living at the time of publication. A separate volume contains a name index.

Who's Who in America. New Providence, NJ: Marquis Who's Who. Annual. This yearly series contains brief biographies of noteworthy living Americans in a variety of fields, listing achievements and home and office addresses. Contains geographic and professional indexes.

Who's Who in American Politics. 2 vols. New Providence, NJ: Bowker. Biennial. This series offers brief biographical summaries of Americans currently active in national, state, and local government. Included are sections representing U.S. holdings: Guam, Puerto

Rico, and the Virgin Islands. Information given for each individual includes party affiliation, offices held, publications, memberships in various organizations, and religion. There is a name index.

Who's Who of American Women. New Providence, NJ: Marquis Who's Who. Biennial. This biographical dictionary surveys notable American women. There is no index.

Reference Books: International Politics and the World

Amnesty International. *Report on Human Rights Around the World.* Alameda, CA: Hunter House. Annual. This volume offers reports on the status of human rights in countries around the world. The entries, organized alphabetically by name of country, include essays, maps, and illustrations dealing with such topics as the use of the death penalty, voting rights and restrictions, and the treatment of minorities. There is no index.

Banks, Arthur S., ed. *Political Handbook of the World.* Binghamton, NY: CSA Publications. The essays in this volume, which is revised every one or two years, summarize the political history and current political situation of a variety of countries, arranged alphabetically. The essays profile political parties, list current government officials by name, and discuss issues such as local media. Also included is a chronology of important political events for the year and UN conferences. There is a general index.

Bowen, Thomas F., and Kelly S. Bowen, eds. *Countries of the World and Their Leaders Yearbook.* 2 vols. Detroit: Gale Research. Annual. This twenty-year-old series prints a variety of information, taken from U.S. State Department reports, relating to selected countries. Each entry includes tables and an essay profiling the country's history, ethnic makeup, and current political condition.

Brune, Lester H. 1981. *Chronological History of United States Foreign Relations: 1776 to January 20, 1981.* 2 vols. New York: Garland. This set of volumes is an extensive time line of events, each briefly summarized, in the history of American foreign policy. Also discussed are international political events that affected U.S. policy. For example, an entry for September 14, 1812, notes the French occupation of Moscow. Volume 2 includes a bibliography of references and a general index. Updated in 1991 with another volume, *Chronological History of U.S. Foreign Relations, January 21, 1981 to January 20, 1991.*

Central Intelligence Agency. *The World Factbook.* Washington, DC: Central Intelligence Agency. Annual. Published primarily for the use of government officials, this CIA compendium gives various kinds of information about different countries. Broad categories, represented by charts and maps as well as by written summaries, include agricultural development, import information, inflation profiles, and population growth. Entries are arranged alphabetically by name of country.

Clements, John. *Clements' Encyclopedia of World Governments.* Dallas: Political Research. Annual. The essays in this series offer analyses of historical events, current government programs, and economic and foreign affairs, among other topics. Each volume includes a chronological listing of important political events occurring during the years surveyed by the volume. There are appendixes and a geographical index.

Demographic Yearbook. New York: United Nations. Annual. This series publishes international demographic statistics from the United Nations. A dual-language text, the volume is printed in French and English. There is a subject index.

The Europa World Year Book. 2 vols. London: Europa. Annual. This publication examines the current status of political, economic, and commercial institutions of different countries. Contents are alphabetized by country, and entries include charts and tables listing vital statistics for each country surveyed.

Flanders, Stephen A., and Carl N. Flanders. 1993. *Dictionary of American Foreign Affairs.* New York: Macmillan. The entries in this volume cover terms, events, documents, and individuals involved with U.S. foreign policy from 1776 to 1993. Appendix A is a useful time line of American foreign affairs. There is a bibliography of references, but no index.

Hunter, Brian, ed. *The Statesman's Yearbook.* New York: St. Martin's. Annual. There are two main divisions, one discussing international organizations, the other profiling countries around the world, summarizing their history and present economic, technical, educational, and cultural status. Each entry includes a bibliography of references. There are three indexes: place and international organizations; products; and names of individuals.

The International Who's Who. London: Europa. Annual. This series offers paragraph-long biographies of notable individuals from different nations. The volumes are not indexed.

Kurian, George Thomas. 1992. *Encyclopedia of the Third World.* 4th ed. 3 vols. New York: Facts on File. For each country surveyed, Kurian compiles data on various factors, including energy, labor, education, law enforcement, history, government, human rights, and foreign policy. Volume 3 includes appendixes, a bibliography of references, and a general index.

Lawson, Edward, and Mary Lou Bertucci. 1996. *Encyclopedia of Human Rights.* New York: Taylor & Francis. Various topics concerning international human rights activities from 1945 to 1990 are discussed, and significant government documents are reprinted, such as the text of the *Convention Relating to the Status of Refugees* (1951). The appendixes include a chronological list of international human rights documents and a list of worldwide human rights institutions. There is a subject index.

Mackie, Thomas T., and Richard Rose. *The International Almanac of Electoral History.* 2d ed. New York: Facts on File. Annual. This volume publishes information, represented in both statistical charts and written analyses, on election results in Western nations from the late nineteenth century to the present. The information is arranged alphabetically by country. There is no index.

Staar, Richard F., ed. *Yearbook on International Communist Affairs.* Stanford, CA: Hoover Institution. Annual through 1991. Communism as it developed in both communist and noncommunist countries is surveyed in this publication. Countries are divided into broad geographical regions and then dealt with alphabetically. There is a name index and a subject index.

The World Almanac and Book of Facts. Mahwah, NJ: World Almanac/Funk & Wagnalls. Annual. This almanac publishes a wide variety of information on the United States and world affairs. Many tables and charts are included. There is an index.

World Debt Tables: External Debt of Developing Countries. Washington, DC: World Bank. Annual. The tables in this volume, summarizing data for the World Bank, break down and analyze debts owed by the developing nations. There is no index.

Other Reference Books

The Index and Abstract Directory: An International Guide to Services and Serials Coverage. 1993. 3d ed. 2 vols. Birmingham, AL: Ebsco. The directory gives information on the over 35,000 serial publications in Ebsco's publishing database. Entries are arranged alphabetically by subject. Included are listings for national and international political science periodicals. There are two indexes: one for titles and one for subjects.

Montney, Charles, ed. *Directories in Print.* Detroit: Gale Research. Annual. According to the introduction to the two-volume 1994 edition, Volume 1 "describes 15,900 directories, rosters, guides, and other print and nonprint address lists published in the United States and worldwide" (vii). Each entry includes address, fax number, price of the directory, and a description of its contents. Arrangement is by subject. Chapter 19 covers "Law, Military, and Government" directories. Volume 2 contains subject and title/ keyword indexes.

Olson, Stan. *The Foundation Directory.* New York: The Foundation Center. Annual. This publication lists and describes over 6,300 foundations with at least $2 million in assets or $200,000 in annual giving. Listed alphabetically by state, each entry includes financial information, names of donors, and brief descriptions of the purpose and activities of the foundation, as well as a list of officers. Indexed.

Wesserman, Paul, ed. *Consumer Sourcebook.* 2 vols. Detroit: Gale Research. Biennial. This guide to information sources for consumers is arranged according to the types of organizations profiled. Subheadings include "Government Organizations," "Information Centers," "Associations," and "Media Services." Contents are indexed by name of organization, subject, and publications put out by the various organizations.

Wiener, Philip P., ed. 1980. *Dictionary of the History of Ideas.* 5 vols. New York: Scribner's. Originally published in 1973–74. The essays in these volumes discuss ideas that have helped to shape and continue to shape human culture. The essays are arranged alphabetically by topic, within a series of broad subheadings. The subheading on politics, for example, includes sixty essays on such topics as "Authority," "Democracy," "Legal Concept of Freedom," "Liberalism," and "Social Attitudes Towards Women." Volume 5 consists of a subject and name index. Digitized and placed on the Web in 2003 by the University of Virginia and maintained by its Electronic Text Center. http://etext.lib.virginia.edu/DicHist/dict.html.

Woy, James, ed. *Encyclopedia of Business Information Sources.* Detroit: Gale Research. Annual. This guide to information on more than 1,100 business topics is arranged by subject and surveys both print and electronic sources, such as on-line databases. Headings include "Customs House," "Government Publications," "Laws," and "United States Congress." There is no index.

Government and Politics Periodicals

Clements' International Report. Dallas: Political Research. This monthly newsletter comprises essays on current international political and historical concerns. There is a biannual subject index.

Congressional Digest. Washington, DC: Government Printing Office. A magazine that selects topics for debate and presents arguments on different sides of the issues.

Congressional Quarterly Weekly Report. Washington, DC: Government Printing Office. A weekly magazine that describes all the major activities of the U.S. House and Senate.

Congressional Record. Washington, DC: Government Printing Office. The official, constitutionally mandated publication of the activities and official documents of Congress.

Federal Register. Washington, DC: Government Printing Office. Daily issues of the Federal Register print the regulations and legal notices issued by federal agencies.

GPO Monthly Catalog of United States Government Publications. Washington, DC: Government Printing Office. This publication includes citations from the annual Periodicals Supplement and the United States Congressional Serial Set Supplement. Topics covered include finance, business, and demographics.

Library of Congress. *Monthly Checklist of State Publications.* Washington, DC: Government Printing Office. This checklist, organized alphabetically by state, lists state documents received by the Library of Congress over the preceding month. There is a subject index.

Office of the Federal Register/ National Archives and Records Administration. *Code of Federal Regulations.* Washington, DC: Government Printing Office. Annual. As explained in the brief introduction to each issue, this mammoth set of volumes, updated yearly, constitutes "a codification of the general and permanent rules published in the Federal Register by the Executive departments and agencies of the Federal Government." The code is divided into fifty "titles," which are, in turn, further subdivided.

PACs & Lobbies. This semimonthly newsletter reports on federal developments affecting campaign finance and lobbying activities.

U.S. Code Congressional and Administrative News. St. Paul, MN: West. Annual. This series of volumes reprints selected laws made during the current session of Congress. A subject index is included.

The United States Law Week: A National Survey of Current Law. Washington, DC: Bureau of National Affairs. This weekly newsletter summarizes important court decisions and prints articles on current legal topics.

World of Politics: Taylor's Encyclopedia of Government Officials, Federal and State. Dallas: Political Research. This monthly newsletter publishes articles discussing responses from the various branches of government to current issues. The periodical is indexed three times a year.

6.2 PERIODICAL INDEXES

Newspaper Indexes

The following major newspapers have indexes available either in print or on microfilm:

The Chicago Tribune	*The New York Times*
The Houston Post	*The Times of London*
The Los Angeles Times	*The Wall Street Journal*
The National Observer	*The Washington Post*
The New Orleans Times-Picayune	

Periodical Indexes

America: History and Life (article abstracts and citations of reviews and dissertations on life in the United States and Canada)
The American Humanities Index
Bibliographic Index
Biography Index
Book Review Index
Book Reviews in Historical Periodicals
Combined Retrospective (an index of the *Journals in Political Science*, 1886–1974; 6 vols.)
Historical Abstracts
Humanities Index
An Index to Book Reviews in the Humanities
Index to U.S. Government Periodicals

International Political Science Abstracts

The New York Times Biographical Service (a monthly compilation of obituaries photocopied from the *New York Times,* arranged chronologically, with an index on the front cover of each issue)

PAIS International in Print (subject index to international periodical articles in the social and political sciences)

Public Affairs Information Service: PAIS

Reader's Guide to Periodical Literature

Social Sciences Index

Sociological Abstracts

Ulrich's International Periodicals Directory, 1993–94 (5 vols.)

United States Political Science Documents

Urban Affairs Abstracts

Weekly Compilation of Presidential Documents (weekly publication including the president's "remarks, news conferences, messages, statements"— all public presidential utterances for that week)

6.3   STATISTICS

Government Finance Statistics Yearbook. Washington, DC: International Monetary Fund. Annual. This reference volume publishes tables that document revenues and spending by governments around the world. There is no index.

Stanley, Harold W., and Richard G. Niemi. 1995. *Vital Statistics on American Politics.* 5th ed. Washington, DC: Congressional Quarterly Press. The charts and tables in this reference guide for political statistics cover a wide range of topics related to American politics, including the media (newspaper endorsements of presidential candidates from 1932 are graphed), interest groups, and the geographical and ethnic makeup of political bodies. There is an index.

Statistical Reference Index Annual: Abstracts. Bethesda, MD: Congressional Information Service. Annual. This volume is a guide to American statistical publications from private organizations and state government sources. Contents are organized by the type of organization publishing the reports. Each publication listed is briefly described in an abstract. An accompanying volume includes four separate indexes: subject and name, category, issuing sources, and title index.

Statistical Yearbook. New York: United Nations. Annual. Published in French and English, this yearly volume summarizes data from several U.N. reports in order to provide an analysis of the world's socioeconomic development over a twelve-month period. Contents are arranged by topic. The book is not indexed.

Statistical Yearbook. Paris: UNESCO. Annual. The statistical charts in this yearly publication cover education, science, and aspects of cultural life for 200 member nations of UNESCO. Material is generated from UNESCO questionnaires answered by a wide variety of respondents. The text is printed in three languages. There is no index.

U.S. Bureau of the Census. *Statistical Abstract of the United States.* Washington, DC: Department of Commerce. Annual. This volume, part of a series published since 1878, summarizes statistics on the country's social, political, and economic organization. There is an index.

Vital Statistics of the United States. 2 vols. Hyattsville, MD: U.S. Department of Health and Human Services. Annual. Each of the two volumes of this yearly series publishes statistics under a different heading. Volume 1 covers natality: tables of the year's birth statistics at the national and local levels and for U.S. holdings. Volume 2 covers mortality: death statistics.

Yearbook of Labour Statistics. Geneva: International Labour Office. Annual. This publication offers statistical tables on the economic development of countries around the world. There is an index of countries.

Statistical and political abstracts are also published by different public and private organizations for each state.

6.4   GOVERNMENT AGENCIES

For most papers you will write in other subjects, such as biology, history, or a foreign language, the library is the place where you will find most if not all of the information you will need. As a student of political science you will most certainly find much valuable information on the library shelves. However, topics in political science afford an unusual opportunity to get information from other sources, because many political science topics require recent information about state and local governments, the U.S. government, and governments of other nations. When topics such as these are assigned or selected, government agencies, research centers, and public interest groups often have more recent and more detailed information than is available in most college and university libraries. In fact, in most cases, for whatever topic you select, someone in a public agency or private organization has probably already conducted significant research on the issue. If you can find the right person, you may be able to secure much more information in much less time than you can by looking in your local library.

Did you know, for example, that the members of the U.S. Senate and House of Representatives constantly use the services of the Congressional Research Service (CRS) and that, upon request to your representative or senator, CRS materials on the topic of your choice may be sent to you? Further, every local, state, and national government agency has employees who are hired primarily to gather information to help their managers make decisions. Much of the research done by these employees is available upon request.

National Government Agencies

Congressional Yellow Book: Who's Who in Congress, Including Committees and Key Staff. Washington, DC: Monitor Leadership Directories. This quarterly publication, which is bound yearly, identifies senators and representatives by state and district, respectively. It lists committee assignments for each member of Congress and gives addresses and phone numbers of congressional committees and staff. State maps show the districts of members of Congress. There is an index of staff.

The Government Directory of Addresses and Telephone Numbers. Detroit: Omnigraphics. Annual. Entries give names, addresses, and phone numbers for national, state, county, and municipal government officials.

Lauber, Daniel. *Government Job Finder.* River Forest, IL: Planning/Communications. Lauber's biennial listing offers tips on how to find a job in national, state, or local government. A list of directories of various agencies is included. There is an index.

Office of the Federal Register/National Archives and Records Administration. *The United States Government Manual.* Washington, DC: Government Printing Office. Annual. A special edition of the *Federal Register,* the volume gives brief descriptions of the agencies of all three branches of the government and peripheral agencies and organizations. The annotations summarize each agency's history and describe its function and activities.

Office of Management and Budget. *Catalog of Federal Domestic Assistance.* Washington, DC: Government Printing Office. Annual. Government programs offering social and economic assistance to citizens are listed and described briefly in this guide. There is an index.

Orvedahl, Jerry A., ed. *Washington Information Directory.* Washington, DC: Congressional Quarterly. This directory, published every two years, lists and describes various kinds of organizations located in Washington, DC. Contents of the book are divided into eighteen chapters, with such titles as "National Security," "Law and Justice," "Advocacy and Public Services," and "Education and Culture." There are separate subject and name indexes, and address lists for foreign embassies and U.S. ambassadors.

Robinson, Judith Schiek. 1998. *Tapping the Government Grapevine: The User-Friendly Guide to U.S. Government Information Sources.* 3d ed. Phoenix: Oryx. Robinson's manual offers practical help on finding information published by the government, including discussions of electronic media, such as CD-ROMs, databases, and electronic bulletin boards. There are chapters on how to access information from each branch of the government. An index is included.

International Agencies

Yearbook of the United Nations. Dordrecht: Martinus Nijhoff. Annual. This publication contains essays describing U.N. participation in various world events.

6.5   PRIVATE RESEARCH ORGANIZATIONS

Baker, Deborah J., ed. 2004. *National Directory of Nonprofit Organizations.* 17th ed. 2 vols. Rockville, MD: The Taft Group. This guide gives brief listings of over 167,000 nonprofit organizations in the United States, citing addresses, phone numbers, and IRS filing status. Volume 1 lists organizations with annual revenues of $100,000 or over; Volume 2 lists organizations with revenues of $25,000 to $99,000. The contents of both volumes are organized alphabetically by title. Included are an activity index and a geographic index.

Daniels, Peggy Kneffel, and Carol A. Schwartz, eds. *Encyclopedia of Associations.* Detroit: Gale Research. Annual. This guide lists entries for approximately 23,000 national and international organizations. Contents are organized into chapters by subject. Typical chapter titles are "Environmental and Agricultural Organizations" and "Legal, Governmental, Public Administration, and Military Organizations." Each entry includes a brief description of the organization's function and the publications available. There are several indexes.

Dresser, Peter D., and Karen Hill, eds. *Research Centers Directory.* Detroit: Gale Research. Annual. More than 11,700 university-related and other nonprofit research organizations are listed and briefly profiled. The entries are listed in sections by topics. Includes four subsections under the general heading "Private and Public Policy and Affairs." There is a subject index and a master index, as well as a supplemental volume.

Maxfield, Doris Morris, ed. 1993. *Charitable Organizations of the U.S.: A Descriptive and Financial Information Guide.* 2d ed. Detroit: Gale Research. Approximately 800 major public charities are profiled in this guide. Information given includes summaries of each organization's history and purpose, its activities and programs, and financial data. There are three indexes: subject, geographic, and personnel.

Wilson, Robert, ed. *American Lobbyists Directory.* Detroit: Gale Research. More than 65,000 registered federal and state lobbyists are listed in this annual guide, along with the businesses they represent. Included are indexes for lobbyists, their organizations, and general subjects and specialties.

Zuckerman, Edward. *Almanac of Federal PACs.* Washington, DC: Amward. Annual. This directory profiles campaign contributions of every political action committee (PAC) that gave $50,000 or more to candidates for election to the U.S. Senate or House of Representatives. PACs are arranged alphabetically within chapters devoted to different target groups. Each entry includes a brief description of the goals and yearly activities of the PAC. There is a name index.

6.6   LIST OF POLITICAL SCIENCE PERIODICALS

Administration and Society
Administrative Science Quarterly
African Affairs
Africa Quarterly
Alternatives: A Journal for World Policy
American Behavioral Scientist
American Journal of International Law
American Journal of Political Science
American Political Science Review
American Politics Quarterly
Annals of the American Academy of Political and Social Science
Armed Forces and Society
Asian Affairs
Asian Quarterly
Asian Survey
Atlantic Community Quarterly

Australian Journal of Politics and History
Australian Journal of Public Administration
Behavioral Science
Behavior Science Research
Black Politician
British Journal of International Studies
British Journal of Law and Society
British Journal of Political Science
Bureaucrat
Campaign and Elections
Canadian Journal of Behavioral Science
Canadian Journal of Political Science
Canadian Public Administration
Canadian Public Policy
China Quarterly
Communist Affairs

Comparative Political Studies
Comparative Politics
Comparative Strategy
Comparative Studies in Society and History
Conflict
Conflict Bulletin
Conflict Management and Peace Science
Conflict Studies
Congress and the Presidency
Contemporary China
Cooperation and Conflict
Daedalus
Democracy
Development and Change
Diplomatic History
Dissent
East European Quarterly
Electoral Studies
Environmental Policy and Law
European Journal of Political Research

European Journal of Political Science
European Studies Review
Experimental Study of Politics
Foreign Affairs
Foreign Policy
General Systems
German Foreign Policy
German Political Studies
Global Political Assessment
Governance: An International Journal of Policy and Administration
Government & Opposition
Government Finance
Growth and Change
Harvard Journal on Legislation
History and Theory
History of Political Thought
Human Organization
Human Relations
Human Rights Review
Indian Journal of Political Science
Indian Journal of Public Administration
Indian Political Science Review
International Affairs
International Development Review
International Interactions
International Journal of Political Education
International Journal of Public Administration
International Organization
International Political Science Review (Revue Internationale de Science Politique)
International Relations
International Review of Social History
International Security
International Studies

International Studies Quarterly
Interpretation: Journal of Political Philosophy
Jerusalem Journal of International Relations
Journal of African Studies
Journal of Applied Behavioral Science
Journal of Asian Studies
Journal of Common Market Studies
Journal of Commonwealth and Comparative Politics
Journal of Conflict Resolution
Journal of Constitutional and Parliamentary Studies
Journal of Contemporary History
Journal of Developing Areas
Journal of Development Studies
Journal of European Integration
Journal of Health Politics, Policy, and Law
Journal of International Affairs
Journal of Japanese Studies
Journal of Law & Politics
Journal of Libertarian Studies
Journal of Modern African Studies
Journal of Modern History
Journal of Peace Research
Journal of Peace Science
Journal of Policy Analysis and Management
Journal of Policy Modeling
Journal of Political and Military Sociology
Journal of Political Economy
Journal of Political Science
Journal of Politics
Journal of Public Policy
Journal of Social History
Journal of Social Issues

Journal of Social, Political, and Economic Studies
Journal of Strategic Studies
Journal of the History of Ideas
Journal of Theoretical Politics
Journal of Urban Analysis
Law and Contemporary Problems
Law and Policy Quarterly
Law & Society Review
Legislative Studies Quarterly
Mathematical Social Sciences
Micropolitics
Middle Eastern Studies
Middle East Journal
Millennium
Modern China
Multivariate Behavioral Research
New Political Science
Orbis: A Journal of World Affairs
Pacific Affairs
Parliamentarian
Parliamentary Affairs
Parliaments, Estates, and Representation
Peace and Change
Peace Research
Perspectives on Political Science
Philosophy & Public Affairs
Philosophy of the Social Sciences
Planning and Administration
Policy Analysis
Policy and Politics
Policy Review
Policy Sciences
Policy Studies Journal
Policy Studies Review
Political Anthropology
Political Behavior
Political Communication and Persuasion
Political Geography Quarterly
Political Psychology
Political Quarterly

Political Science
Political Science Quarterly
Political Science Review
Political Science Reviewer
Political Studies
Political Theory
Politics
Politics & Society
Polity
Presidential Studies
    Quarterly
Public Administration
    (Australia)
Public Administration
    (United States)
Public Administration
    Review
Public Choice
Public Finance
Public Finance Quarterly
Public Interest
Public Law
Public Opinion Quarterly
Public Policy
Publius: The Journal of
    Federalism
Quarterly Journal of
    Administration
Res Publica
Review of International Studies
    (formerly British Journal
    of International Studies)

Review of Law and Social
    Change
Review of Politics
Revolutionary World
Round Table
Russian Review
Scandinavian Political
    Studies
Science and Public Affairs
Science and Public Policy
Science and Society
Simulation and Games
Slavic Review
Slavonic and East European
    Review
Social Forces
Social Indicators Research
Socialism and Democracy
Social Policy
Social Praxis
Social Research
Social Science Journal
Social Science Quarterly
Social Science Research
Social Theory and Practice
Sociological Analysis and
    Theory
Sociological Methods and
    Research
Sociology and Social Research
Southeastern Political Science
    Review

Soviet Review
Soviet Studies
Soviet Union
Strategic Review
Studies in Comparative
    Communism
Studies in Comparative Inter-
    national Development
Survey
Talking Politics
Technological Forecasting
    and Social Change
Terrorism
Theory and Decision
Theory and Society
Third World
Urban Affairs Quarterly
Urban Studies
War & Society
Washington Quarterly: A
    Review of Strategic and
    International Studies
Western Political Quarterly
West European Politics
Wilson Quarterly
Women & Politics: A Quar-
    terly Journal of Research
    and Policy Studies
World Development
World Policy Journal
World Politics
Youth and Society

◆ CHAPTER 7 ◆
Internet Resources

7.1   WRITING RESOURCES ON THE INTERNET

The preceding chapters of this book have given you much information about research and writing, but the Internet offers even more. A particularly good place to start your Internet search is your own college's On-Line Writing Lab (OWL). Purdue University's OWL, for example may be found at http://owl. english.purdue.edu/. The Purdue OWL home page features many sources of help for people *in the Purdue community,* such as the following:

- One-on-one *tutorials*
- In-lab and in-class *workshops*
- *Study materials* for English as a Second Language
- Conversation groups for English practice
- A grammar hotline
- A collection of reference materials
- Computers and a printer
- Quiet space to study

Purdue's OWL also, however, offers the following resources for *everyone:*

- The Writing Lab Newsletter (including on-line archives of back issues)
- Resources for teachers on using the Writing Lab and OWL, including using OWL in the new English 106/108 course
- Writing Across the Curriculum resources

Your local OWL will also direct you to many more Internet writing resources.

7.2   POLITICS AND GOVERNMENT RESOURCES ON THE INTERNET

Even large catalogs can no longer hold all the potential Internet resources for politics, government, and political science. Fortunately, many Internet sites specialize in creating lists of links to excellent resources. Our purpose in this chapter is to help you locate a few good sites that will in turn lead you to thousands of sources of information for your government and politics research projects.

Internet sources of information about government and politics may be organized into three major groups:

1. Government agencies
2. Universities, private interest groups, and research organizations
3. News agencies

Government Agencies

The very best place to start for information about American government agencies is Thomas (thomas.loc.gov/). Named for President Thomas Jefferson, Thomas is the home page for Congress. It provides dozens of direct links to representatives, senators, legislation, committees, and historical documents, and links to the executive and judicial branches and state and local government agencies as well.

When you choose the Thomas link labeled "Executive Branch," you arrive at a page entitled "Official US Executive Branch Web Sites." Here you may choose from links to agencies in the executive branch of the federal government. While the links on the Thomas page change frequently, as of this writing the list of Executive Branch links begins with the "Executive Office of the President (EOP)," immediately under which are listed the following links:

- White House
- Office of Management and Budget (OMB)
- United States Trade Representative (USTR)

Following these links are a series under the heading "Executive Agencies," comprised of the following links:

- Department of Agriculture (USDA)
- Department of Commerce (DOC)
- Department of Defense (DOD)
- Department of Education
- Department of Energy
- Department of Health and Human Services (HHS)
- Department of Homeland Security (DHS)
- Department of Housing and Urban Development (HUD)
- Department of the Interior (DOI)
- Department of Justice (DOJ)
- Department of Labor (DOL)
- Department of State (DOS)
- Department of Transportation (DOT)
- Department of the Treasury
- Department of Veterans Affairs

Each of these departmental links in turn provides a list of links to organizations within the department. Among the seven links listed under the "Department of Homeland Security (DHS)," for instance, are links to the Bureau of Citizenship and Immigration Services and Customs & Border Protection.

The next major section of the page lists links under the heading "Independent Agencies." There you can find links to 63 government organizations, including the Central Intelligence Agency (CIA), the Federal Trade Commission (FTC), and the National Endowment for the Arts (NEA). Following "Independent Agencies" are the headings "Boards, Commissions, and Committees" and "Quasi-Official Agencies."

If you click on any of these Thomas page links you will arrive at the home page for that specific department, agency, commission, or bureau, which will, in turn guide you to further information.

Of course, the above sites are only the tip of the government Web site iceberg. At the end of this chapter, we will list some helpful Internet resources for information about political science.

If you return to Thomas and select the link named "Judicial Branch," you find yourself confronting links for the Law Library of Congress that provide a wide array of information about courts, laws, and the legal system. Some of the major topics thoroughly covered in these links are:

- The Constitution of the United States
- The U.S. Code and public laws
- State statutes
- Government regulations
- Judicial opinions for federal and state courts
- Court rules
- Controller general decisions
- Executive branch legal materials
- Law journals
- Law-related Internet sites

Universities, Private Interest Groups, and Research Organizations

The second major category of sources of information about politics and government includes universities, private interest groups, and research organizations. Many college political science departments provide Internet sites that feature links to thousands of politics and government sites. The Lehman Social Sciences Library site at Columbia University is a good example (http://www.columbia.edu/cu/lweb/indiv/lehman/guides/uspolitics.html).

Public interest groups also provide a great deal of information on political issues. However, as you search these sites, you must be aware that these groups are in existence to promote a cause and may or may not provide a balanced view of any particular issue. The following list is but a very small list of examples of the hundreds of public interest groups in the United States:

American Association of Retired Persons (AARP)
Amnesty International
Christian Coalition
Environmental Defense Fund
Greenpeace International
National Association of Arab Americans
National Gay and Lesbian Task Force
National Organization for Women (NOW)
National Rifle Association (NRA)
National Right to Life
Planned Parenthood
Sierra Club
Vietnam Veterans of America

In addition to the above-listed public interest groups, there are many "think tanks," or private research organizations, that provide high-quality political, economic, and social analyses. Links to some of these organizations may be found by selecting the "Think Tanks" link at the Kennedy School of Government OPIN site described previously.

News Agencies

The third major category of Internet resources for government and politics includes hundreds of news organizations around the world. CNN, *U.S. News and World Report,* and dozens of other major journalistic ventures provide enormous amounts of information. For example, the *New York Times,* in addition to all its regular news coverage, features a page entitled "Politics Navigator," by Rich Meislin (www.nytimes.com/ref/politics/POLI_NAVI.html). This page contains dozens of links to good sources of information about national, international, state, and local political events, trends, and resources.

7.3 POLITICAL SCIENCE RESOURCES ON THE INTERNET

The first site to visit for political science resources is the home page of the American Political Science Association (APSA), the largest organization of professional political scientists in the world. You will find it at http://www.apsanet.org/. On this page you will find links to the following types of resources, and more.

- Departments of Political Science
- Political Science Organizations
- Scholarly Journals
- Political Science Conferences
- Grants and Fellowships

These links lead to dozens of departments, organizations, conferences, journals, and other sources of information about the discipline of political science.

7.4   ASSESSING THE QUALITY OF INTERNET SOURCES

How do you know if the material you have found in a particular magazine article, Web site, or book is trustworthy? Just because the material has been published does not necessarily make it accurate or fair. Before you consider using any source material, answer the following questions about it:

- *Who is its author?* Is he or she an acknowledged expert in the field? Can you find out anything about the author's credentials? From your reading of the text, what do you feel is the author's personal attitude or bias toward the topic? Say you are researching the practical possibilities of banning smoking in all municipal buildings in your city. Whose data on second-hand smoke would you have more confidence in, data from a study funded by the tobacco industry or data from a study funded by an independent consumer group?
- *Who is the publisher?* Readers generally consider university presses more academically sound than popular presses. University presses usually submit the material they publish to rigorous scrutiny by experts in the field. Popular presses do not always do this. And, because profit is a more demanding goal for popular presses than for university presses, which are subsidized by their universities, material published by popular presses may sometimes sacrifice evenhandedness for the sensationalism that sells.
- *Does the source you are evaluating contain a bibliography?* If not, how will you know if the author's assertions are based on solid scholarship?
- *How old is the source?* Always check the date of publication. An extensive work on the relationship of the United States to Russia published before 1989 may well have lost much of its usefulness in the intervening decade and a half.
- *For whom is the source written?* Scholars usually write for a specific audience. A book on presidential elections of the nineteenth century written for high school history students may simplify its material in a way that would make it unsuitable for the senatorial staff your article is going to brief. Most texts give away their target audience in the first few paragraphs, and you need to be sensitive to your source author's understanding of his or her audience.

It is extremely important that you ask these questions of Internet sources as well as print sources. The growth of the Internet has allowed anyone with a computer and a cause to establish a Web site on virtually any subject imaginable. How do you know whether the Web site you are evaluating reflects evenhanded, knowledgeable scholarship or enthusiastic, poorly researched partisan opinion? One extra tip, in addition to the ones listed above, is to check the three-character extension to the Web site's URL (its Uniform Resource Locator, commonly known as its Web address). A "com" extension normally refers to a commercial (for profit) organization. An "org" extension (normally) refers to a not-for-profit organization.

The extension "gov" refers to United States government agencies. Other countries have their own extensions: www.lemonde.fr., for example, is francc's *Le Monde* Newspaper.

Finally reflect on the potentially varying degrees of Web site reliability that might be indicated by the following site extensions:

.com = commercial
.edu = educational
.mil = military
.org = nonprofit organization
.gov = U.S. government
.net = network

◆ CHAPTER 8 ◆
Book Reviews and Article Critiques

8.1 BOOK REVIEWS

Successful book reviews answer three questions:

- What did the writer of the book try to communicate?
- How clearly and convincingly did he or she get this message across to the reader?
- Was the message worth reading?

Capable book reviewers of several centuries have answered these three questions well. People who read a book review want to know if a particular book is worth reading, for their own particular purposes, before buying or reading it. These potential readers want to know the book's subject and its strengths and weaknesses, and they want to gain this information as easily and quickly as possible. Your goal in writing a book review, therefore, is to help people efficiently decide whether to buy or read a book. Your immediate objectives may be to please your instructor and get a good grade, but these objectives are most likely to be met if you focus on a book review's audience: people who want help in selecting books to buy or read. In the process of writing a book review that reaches this primary goal, you will also:

- Learn about the book you are reviewing
- Learn about professional standards for book reviews in political science
- Learn the essential steps of book reviewing that apply to any academic discipline

This final objective, learning to review a book properly, has more applications than you may at first imagine. First, it helps you to focus quickly on the essential elements of a book, and to draw from a book its informational value for yourself and others. Some of the most successful people in government, business, and the professions speed-read several books a week, more for the knowledge they contain than for enjoyment. These readers then apply this knowledge to substantial advantage in their professions. It is normally not wise to speed-read a book you are reviewing because you are unlikely to gain enough information to evaluate it fairly from such a fast reading. Writing book reviews, however, helps you to become proficient in quickly sorting out valuable information from material that is not. The ability to make such discriminations is a fundamental ingredient in management and professional success.

In addition, writing book reviews for publication allows you to participate in the discussions of the broader intellectual and professional community of which you are a part. People in law, medicine, teaching, engineering, administration, and other fields are frequently asked to write book reviews to help others assess newly released publications.

Before beginning your book review, read the following sample. It is Gregory M. Scott's review of *Political Islam: Revolution, Radicalism, or Reform?*, edited by John L. Esposito. The review appeared in volume 26 of the *Southeastern Political Science Review* (June 1998), and is reprinted here by permission:

> Behold an epitaph for the specter of monolithically autocratic Islam. In its survey of Islamic political movements from Pakistan to Algeria, *Political Islam: Revolution, Radicalism, or Reform?* effectively lays to rest the popular notion that political expressions of Islam are inherently violent and authoritarian. For this accomplishment alone John L. Esposito and company's scholarly anthology merits the attention of serious students of religion and politics, and justifies the book's own claim to making a "seminal contribution." Although it fails to identify how Islam as religious faith and cultural tradition lends Muslim politics a distinctively Islamic flavor, this volume clearly answers the question posed by its title: yes, political Islam encompasses not only revolution and radicalism, but moderation and reform as well.
>
> Although two of the eleven contributors are historians, *Political Islam* exhibits both the strengths and weaknesses of contemporary political science with respect to religion. It identifies connections between economics and politics, and between culture and politics, much better than it deciphers the nuances of the relationships between politics and religious belief. After a general introduction, the first three articles explore political Islam as illegal opposition, first with a summary of major movements and then with studies of Algeria and the Gulf states. In her chapter entitled "Fulfilling Prophecies: State Policy and Islamist Radicalism," Lisa Anderson sets a methodological guideline for the entire volume when she writes:
>
> > Rather than look to the substance of Islam or the content of putatively Islamic political doctrines for a willingness to embrace violent means to desired ends, we might explore a different perspective and examine the political circumstances, or institutional environment, that breeds political radicalism, extremism, or violence independent of the content of the doctrine (18).
>
> Therefore, rather than assessing how Islam as religion affects Muslim politics, all the subsequent chapters proceed to examine politics, economics, and culture in a variety of Muslim nations. This means that the title of the book is slightly misleading: it discusses Muslim politics rather than political Islam. Esposito provides the book's conclusion about the effects of Islamic belief on the political process when he maintains that "the appeal to religion is a two-edged sword. . . . It can provide or enhance self-legitimation, but it can also be used as a yardstick for judgment by opposition forces and delegitimation" (70).

The second part of the volume features analyses of the varieties of political processes in Iran, Sudan, Egypt, and Pakistan. These chapters clearly demonstrate not only that Islamic groups may be found in varied positions on normal economic and ideological spectrums, but that Islam is not necessarily opposed to moderate, pluralist politics. The third section of the anthology examines the international relations of Hamas, Afghani Islamists, and Islamic groups involved in the Middle East peace process. These chapters are especially important for American students because they present impressive documentation for the conclusions that the motives and demands of many Islamic groups are considerably more moderate and reasonable than much Western political commentary would suggest.

The volume is essentially well written. All the articles with the exception of chapter two avoid unnecessarily dense political science jargon. As a collection of methodologically sound and analytically astute treatments of Muslim politics, *Political Islam: Revolution, Radicalism, or Reform?* is certainly appropriate for adoption as a supplemental text for courses in religion and politics. By way of noting what it does not cover, readers may consider that although it is sufficient for its purposes as it stands, the volume could be a primary text in a course on Islamic politics if it included four additional chapters:

1. an historical overview of the origins and varieties of Islam as religion
2. a summary of the global Islamic political-ideological spectrum (from liberal to fundamentalist)
3. an overview of the varieties of global Islamic cultures
4. an attempt to describe in what manner, if any, Islam, in all its varieties, gives politics a different flavor from the politics of other major religions.

Elements of a Book Review

Book reviews in political science contain the same essential elements of all book reviews. Because political science is nonfiction, book reviews within the discipline focus less on a work's writing style and more on its content and method than do reviews of fiction. Your book review should generally contain four basic elements, although not always in this order:

1. Enticement
2. Examination
3. Elucidation
4. Evaluation

Enticement

Your first sentence should entice people to read your review. A crisp summary of what the book is about entices your reader because it lets her know that you can quickly and clearly come to the point. She knows that her time and efforts will not be wasted in an attempt to wade through your vague prose in hopes of finding out something about the book. Notice Scott's opening line: "Behold an epitaph for the specter of monolithically autocratic Islam." It is a bit overburdened with large words, but it is engaging and precisely sums up the essence of the review. Your opening statement can be engaging and "catchy," but be sure that it provides an accurate portrayal of the book in one crisp statement.

Examination

Your book review should allow the reader to join you in examining the book. Tell the reader what the book is about. One of the greatest strengths of Scott's review is that his first paragraph immediately tells you exactly what he thinks the book accomplishes.

When you review a book, write about what is actually in the book, not what you think is probably there or ought to be there. Do not explain how you would have written the book, but instead how the author wrote it. Describe the book in clear, objective terms. Tell enough about the content to identify the author's major points.

Elucidation

Elucidate, or clarify, the book's value and contribution to political science by defining (1) what the author is attempting to do, and (2) how the author's work fits within current similar efforts in the discipline of political science or scholarly inquiry in general. Notice how Scott immediately describes what Esposito is trying to do: "This volume clearly answers the question posed by its title." Scott precedes this definition of the author's purpose by placing his work within the context of current similar writing in political science by stating that "for this accomplishment alone John L. Esposito and company's scholarly anthology merits the attention of serious students of religion and politics, and justifies the book's own claim to making a 'seminal contribution.'"

The elucidation portion of book reviews often provides additional information about the author. Scott has not included such information about Esposito in his review, but it would be helpful to know, for example, if Esposito has written other books on the subject, has developed a reputation for exceptional expertise on a certain issue, or is known to have a particular ideological bias. How would your understanding of this book be changed, for example, if you knew that its author were a leader of Hamas or the PLO? Include information in your book review about the author that helps the reader understand how this book fits within the broader concerns of political science.

Evaluation

Once you explain what the book is attempting to do, you should tell the reader the extent to which this goal has been met. To evaluate a book effectively, you will need to establish evaluation criteria and then compare the book's content to those criteria. You do not need to define your criteria specifically in your review, but they should be evident to the reader. Your criteria will vary according to the book you are reviewing, and you may discuss them in any order that is helpful to the reader. Consider, however, including the following among the criteria that you establish for your book review:

- How important is the subject to the study of politics and government?
- How complete and thorough is the author's coverage of the subject?
- How carefully is the author's analysis conducted?
- What are the strengths and limitations of the author's methodology?

- What is the quality of the writing? Is it clear, precise, and interesting?
- How does this book compare with others on the subject?
- What contribution does this book make to political science?
- Who will enjoy or benefit from this book?

When giving your evaluations according to these criteria, be specific. If you write, "This is a good book; I liked it very much," you have told the reader nothing of interest or value. Notice, however, how Scott's review helps to clearly define the content and the limitations of the book by contrasting the volume with what he describes as an ideal primary text for a course in Islamic politics: "By way of noting what it does not cover, readers may consider that although it is sufficient for its purposes as it stands, the volume could be a primary text in a course on Islamic politics if it included four additional chapters."

Qualities of Effective Political Science Book Reviews

Effective political science book reviews:

- Serve the reader
- Are fair
- Are concise and specific, not vague and general

Write your review with the potential reader, not yourself or the book's author, in mind. The person who may read the book is, in a manner of speaking, your client.

Your reader wants a fair review of the book. Do not be overly generous to a book of poor quality, but do not be too critical of an honest effort to tackle a very complex or difficult problem. If you have a bias that may affect your review, let your reader know this, but do so briefly. Do not shift the focus from the book's ideas to your own. Do not attack a work because of the author's politics. Do not chide the author for not having written a book different from the one he or she has written.

The reader of your book review is not interested in your thoughts about politics or other subjects. Try to appreciate the author's efforts and goals, and sympathize with the author, but remain sufficiently detached to identify errors. Try to show the book's strengths and weaknesses as clearly as possible.

Write a review that is interesting, appealing, and even charming, but not at the expense of accuracy or of the book being reviewed. Be erudite but not prolix. (To be *erudite* is to display extensive knowledge. To be *prolix* is to be wordy and vague.) Your goal is to display substantial knowledge of the book's content, strengths, and weaknesses in as few words as possible.

Preliminaries: Before Writing a Book Review

Before sitting down to write your review, make sure you do the following:

- *Get further directions from your instructor.* Ask if there are specific directions beyond those in this manual for the number of pages or the content of the review.

- *Read the book.* Reviewers who skim or merely read a book's jacket do a great disservice to the author. Read the book thoroughly.
- *Respond to the book.* As you read, make notes on your responses to the book. Organize them into the categories of enticement, examination, elucidation, and evaluation.
- *Get to know the subject.* Use the library to find a summary of works on the issue. Such a summary may be found in a review in a journal or in a recent textbook on the subject.
- *Familiarize yourself with other books by the author.* If the author has written other works, learn enough about them to be able to describe them briefly to your readers.
- *Read reviews of other political science books.* Many political science journals have book review sections, usually at the end of an issue. Go to the library and browse through some of the reviews in several journals. Not only will you get to know what is expected from a political science book review, but you will find many interesting ideas on how books are approached and evaluated.

Format and Content

The directions for writing papers provided in Chapters 1 through 3 apply to book reviews as well. Some further instructions specific to book reviews are needed, however. First, list on the title page, along with the standard information required for political science papers, data on the book being reviewed: title, author, place and name of publisher, date, and number of pages. As the sample that follows shows, the title of the book should be in italics or underlined, but not both:

Shoveling Smoke

A Clay Parker Crime Novel

by

Austin Davis

San Francisco: Chronicle Books

2003. 256 pages.

reviewed by

Constance Squires

POL 213

Dr. Christopher Givan

Central Mideastern University

January 1, 2006

Reflective or Analytical Book Reviews

Instructors in the humanities and social sciences normally assign two types of book reviews: the *reflective* and the *analytical. Ask your instructor which type of book review you are to write.* The purpose of a reflective book review is for the student reviewer to exercise creative analytical judgment without being influenced by the reviews of others. Reflective book reviews contain all the elements covered in this chapter—enticement, examination, elucidation, and evaluation—but they do not include the views of others who have also read the book.

Analytical book reviews contain all the information provided by reflective reviews but add an analysis of the comments of other reviewers. The purpose is thus to review not only the book itself but also its reception in the professional community.

To write an analytical book review, insert a review analysis section immediately after your summary of the book. To prepare this section, use the *Book Review Digest* and *Book Review Index* in the library to locate other reviews of the book that have been published in journals and other periodicals. As you read these reviews:

1. List the criticisms of the book's strengths and weaknesses that are made in the reviews.
2. Develop a concise summary of these criticisms, indicate the overall positive or negative tone of the reviews, and mention some of the most commonly found comments.
3. Evaluate the criticisms found in these reviews. Are they basically accurate in their assessment of the book?
4. Write a review analysis of two pages or less that states and evaluates steps 2 and 3 above, and place it in your book review immediately after your summary of the book.

Length of a Book Review

Unless your instructor gives you other directions, a reflective book review should be three to five typed pages in length, and an analytical book review should be five to seven pages long. In either case, a brief, specific, concise book review is almost always preferred over one of greater length.

8.2   ARTICLE CRITIQUES

An *article critique* is a paper that evaluates an article published in an academic journal. A good critique tells the reader what point the article is trying to make and how convincingly it makes this point. Writing an article critique achieves three purposes. First, it provides you with an understanding of the information contained in a scholarly article and a familiarity with other information written on the same topic. Second, it provides you with an opportunity to apply and develop your critical thinking skills as you attempt to evaluate critically a political scientist's work. Third, it helps you to improve your own writing skills as you attempt to describe the selected article's strengths and weaknesses so that your readers can clearly understand them.

The first step in writing an article critique is to select an appropriate article. Unless your instructor specifies otherwise, select an article from a scholarly journal (such as the *American Political Science Review, Journal of Politics,* or *Southeastern Political Science Review*) and not a popular or journalistic publication (such as *Time* or the *National Review*). Chapter 6 of this manual includes a substantial list of academic political science journals, but your instructor may also accept appropriate articles from academic journals in other disciplines, such as history, economics, or sociology.

Choosing an Article

Three other considerations should guide your choice of an article. First, browse article titles until you find a topic that interests you. Writing a critique will be much more satisfying if you have an interest in the topic. Hundreds of interesting journal articles are published every year. The following articles, for example, appeared in the Spring 2004 (6:1) issue of the *Hedgehog Review:*

"Religion and Violence"

Introduction	The Puzzle of Religion and Violence
René Girard	Violence and Religion: Cause or Effect?
Mark Juergensmeyer	Is Religion the Problem?
William T. Cavanaugh	Sins of Omission: What "Religion and Violence" Arguments Ignore
Slavica Jakelic	Religion, Collective Identity, and Violence in Bosnia and Herzegovina
Khaled Abou El Fadl	Speaking, Killing, and Loving in God's Name
Thomas Cushman	A Conversation on Religion and Violence with Veena Das
Jennifer L. Geddes	Peacemaking among the Abrahamic Faiths: An Interview with Peter Ochs
Justin S. Holcomb	A Review of Anna Lännström's *Promise and Peril*
Charles K. Bellinger	Religion and Violence: A Bibliography

The second consideration in selecting an article is your current level of knowledge. Many political science studies, for example, employ sophisticated statistical techniques. You may be better prepared to evaluate them if you have studied statistics.

The third consideration is to select a current article, one written within the last twelve months. Most material in political science is quickly superseded by new studies. Selecting a recent study will help ensure that you will be engaged in an up-to-date discussion of your topic.

Writing the Critique

Once you have selected and carefully read your article, you may begin to write your critique, which will cover five areas:

1. Thesis
2. Methods
3. Evidence of thesis support
4. Contribution to the literature
5. Recommendation

Thesis

Your first task is to find and clearly state the thesis of the article. The thesis is the main point the article is trying to make. In a 1997 article entitled "Unequal Participation: Democracy's Unresolved Dilemma," APSA president Arend Lijphart, Research Professor of Political Science at the University of California, San Diego, states his thesis very clearly:

> Low voter turnout is a serious democratic problem for five reasons: (1) It means unequal turnout that is systematically biased against less well-to-do citizens. (2) Unequal turnout spells unequal political influence. (3) U.S. voter turnout is especially low, but, measured as percent of voting-age population, it is also relatively low in most other countries. (4) Turnout in midterm, regional, local, and supranational elections—less salient but by no means unimportant elections—tends to be especially poor. (5) Turnout appears to be declining everywhere.

Many authors, however, do not present their theses this clearly. After you have read the article, ask yourself whether you had to hunt for the thesis. Comment about the clarity of the author's thesis presentation and state the author's thesis in your critique. Before proceeding with the remaining elements of your critique, consider the importance of the topic. Has the author written something that is important for us as citizens or political scientists to read?

Methods

In your critique, carefully answer the following questions: What methods did the author use to investigate the topic? In other words, how did the author go about supporting the thesis? Were the appropriate methods used? Did the author's approach to supporting the thesis make sense? Did the author employ the selected methods correctly? Did you discover any errors in the way he or she conducted the research?

Evidence of Thesis Support

In your critique, answer the following questions: What evidence did the author present in support of the thesis? What are the strengths of the evidence presented? What are the weaknesses of the evidence? On balance, how well did the author support the thesis?

Contribution to the Literature

This step will probably require you to undertake some research of your own. Using the research resources discussed in Chapters 6 and 7 of this manual, identify articles and books published on the subject of your selected article within the past five years. Browse the titles and read perhaps half a dozen of the publications that appear to provide the best discussion of the topic. In your critique, list the most important other articles or books that have been published on your topic and then, in view of these publications, evaluate the contribution that your selected article makes to a better understanding of the subject.

Recommendation

In this section of your critique, summarize your evaluation of the article. Tell your readers several things: Who will benefit from reading this article? What will the benefit be? How important and extensive is that benefit? Clearly state your evaluation of the article in the form of a thesis for your own critique. Your thesis might be something like the following:

> Arend Lijphart's article entitled "Unequal Participation: Democracy's Unresolved Dilemma" is the most concise and comprehensive discussion of the problem of unequal participation published in recent years. Political scientists should conscientiously confront Lijphart's warning because he conclusively demonstrates that unequal participation presents an imminent threat to American democracy.

When writing this assignment, follow the directions for paper formats in Chapter 3 of this manual. Ask your instructor for directions concerning the length of the critique, but in the absence of further guidelines, your paper should not exceed five pages (typed, double-spaced).

◆ CHAPTER 9 ◆
Traditional Research Papers

9.1 DEFINITION: TRADITIONAL STUDIES IN POLITICAL SCIENCE

The word *traditional* does not have a fixed or precise meaning in political science today. When we write traditional papers in political science, however, we normally utilize both of the following:

1. The traditional approach to the study of politics (as described in the Introduction to this manual and below)
2. The traditional format for papers (as described in Chapter 3)

Traditional papers in political science attempt to help readers understand political actors, events, trends, institutions, or movements. They explain the context, precedents, causes, conditions, and outcomes of political activity. They usually focus on one or more aspects of political life:

- History
- Biography, leadership, management, or personality
- Institutions
- Constitutions, laws, and legislation
- Issues
- Philosophies, theories, methods, and concepts such as freedom, justice, and equality

It is important to note that what is considered "traditional" keeps changing over time. For example, in the early 1960s, Gabriel Almond's use of the term *political socialization* and David Easton's use of the term *political system* were considered to be departures from "traditional" political science concepts. Today, however, these concepts have been so widely adopted that they and similar terms are used in standard discourse within the traditional approach.

Many traditional studies in political science focus on the ways that a single individual affects and responds to the political environment. Such works most often take the form of biographies and studies of leadership, management styles, and personalities. For example, numerous biographies and autobiographies of American presidents are published before, during, and after their terms of office. These studies normally attempt to draw conclusions about the nature of politics, leadership, or power. Reflecting on his own years as president, Jimmy Carter has this to say:

> Although I was surrounded by people eager to help me, my most vivid impression of the Presidency remains the loneliness in which the most difficult decisions had to be made. As a matter of fact, very few easy ones came to my desk. If the answers to a question were obvious, they were provided in a city hall or a state capitol. If they involved national or international affairs and were not particularly controversial, decisions were made at some lower level in government. . . . And I prayed a lot—more than ever before in my life—asking God to give me a clear mind, sound judgment, and wisdom in dealing with affairs that could affect the lives of so many people in our country and around the world. (Carter 1982, 61–62)

Regardless of whether traditional studies in political science focus primarily on individuals, institutions, laws, constitutions, or political concepts such as freedom, order, or justice, they almost always describe their subjects within their historical, legal, and political contexts and attempt to evaluate them with the help of values or standards such as "the public interest" or "constitutionality."

9.2   TRADITIONAL POLITICAL SCIENCE RESEARCH PAPERS

The Audience for the Traditional Political Science Paper

One of the fundamental considerations for a writer is the intended audience. In writing policy analysis papers, for example, the author's first consideration is the person or group that has commissioned the study. The question of audience, however, rarely comes up in discussions of the traditional political science paper, perhaps because the audience is assumed. It is unfortunate that this assumption is not often examined.

Who is the audience for most traditional political science papers? The answer is *students of political science*. This group is usually comprised of three types of "students": (1) the instructor who assigned the paper and who will read it primarily to evaluate the writer's understanding; (2) college or university students who will hear the paper discussed in a seminar or may read it for their own research needs; and perhaps even (3) the general public, who will read it to enhance their understanding of a topic they find to be of interest.

The Four Components of Traditional Political Science Papers

Before writing your traditional paper, be sure to read Chapters 1 and 2. This will save you a good deal of time. You will find there is not one set pattern or process for writing papers. Certain basic tasks need to be completed, but you must experiment to find out how you can best accomplish them. Remember that traditional papers are meant to explain some aspect of politics or government, which they do by (1) stating a thesis, and (2) supporting that thesis with appropriate documentation. To perform these two tasks, traditional papers normally include four basic types of information:

- A specific *definition* of the topic or subject of the paper
- A discussion of the historical, legal, and institutional *context* of the subject
- A careful *description* of the subject
- A concluding *evaluation* of the subject

Definition

A precise *definition* of a paper's subject is often the most difficult part to write. Suppose that you are studying the development of presidential power during the twentieth century in order to understand how such power works. You must at some point define presidential power. Is it the expressly granted powers of the Constitution? Is it the power to persuade? Is it the growing bureaucracy over which the president has some control?

Context

The historical, legal, and institutional *context* of the subject of a paper is normally an important part of a traditional study in political science. To continue with our example, the development of presidential power during the twentieth century can be understood only if certain facts influencing its development are also known. What effect did the Great Depression, for example, have on President Roosevelt's ability to change government social welfare policies? What portions of the Constitution allowed twentieth-century presidents to assume powers they had not exercised previously? What effect did public media technology have on presidents' ability to influence votes?

Description

The *description* of the subject is the largest component of many traditional studies. A paper on the development of presidential power during the twentieth century would spend considerable time describing the manner in which this power has been expanded, probably giving numerous examples from most if not all of the presidencies of the century.

Evaluation

The *evaluation* is a challenging element of traditional papers. Merely listing facts about presidents and their exercise of power, for example, would normally not be sufficient; you would instead need to show that you are capable of drawing conclusions from the materials you have studied. In what respects has presidential power increased? What factors contributed the most to this increase? In what ways is presidential power more limited now than it was in 1900?

Evaluation takes place in two steps. The first step is to establish evaluation criteria. Applied to our example, this means that you must identify the phenomena that would indicate the existence and degree of change in presidential power. You might examine the change in public opinion polls before and after presidential addresses, or count the number of presidentially sponsored bills passed by Congress.

The second step is to apply the evaluation criteria that you have selected and draw conclusions from the results. If, for example, you find a greater increase in presidential popularity after the addresses of President Clinton than after those of President Bush, what does this mean to your overall assessment of presidential power in the twentieth century? The conclusion to your traditional political science paper will normally be your interpretation of the results of your evaluation of your subject. Your conclusion, therefore, will clearly restate your thesis and the evidence that you have gathered for its support. It should also include any insights that you have gained in the process of writing your paper.

Steps in Writing a Traditional Political Science Paper

When writing your traditional political science paper, follow the suggestions in Chapters 1 through 7. Traditional papers may be written on many subjects and may emphasize different aspects of these subjects. *Be sure to ask your instructor to clarify the assignment before you begin.* You are most likely to write a good paper if you thoughtfully consider the appropriate role that each of the four basic elements of traditional papers will play: a specific *definition* of the topic; a discussion of the historical, legal, and institutional *context* of the subject; a careful *description* of the subject; and a concluding *evaluation* of the subject.

Finding a Topic for a Traditional Political Science Paper

Topics for traditional papers in political science may come from all areas of the discipline. Before beginning your search, read the guidelines for selecting a topic presented in Chapter 1. *Ask your instructor for specific advice on what is appropriate for the course.*

◆ CHAPTER 10 ◆

Writing to Communicate and Act

10.1   LETTERS TO NEWSPAPER EDITORS

A letter to a newspaper editor is neither an exercise in creative writing nor a philosophical thought piece. Its audience is not the editor so much as the general public, for your goal in writing the letter is to get it published in the newspaper so that you can influence the opinions of others. Because your aim is publication, remember that most letters that are actually published are responses to a specific editorial, article, or letter that has already (and recently) appeared in the paper. Successful letters to the editor, therefore, are well written statements that

- Point out and then correct inaccurate, false, or misleading information in a recently printed news item, editorial, or letter
- Supplement, reinforce, refute, or clarify a recently printed statement with new information
- Offer a new point of view on a current issue or a recently printed statement

How Do I Find a Topic?

On the shelves of the periodicals room of your college library you will find the last several issues of your local newspaper. Read through them, looking for articles or other items that particularly interest you. Can you find something that you feel passionate about? Pay special attention to letters to the editor. Note the types of letters that the newspaper is printing. Are they long or short? Are they well balanced or do they tend to be incendiary? Find a specific news article, editorial, or letter to the editor that interests you personally and that you believe is of interest to people in your community. Examine the article carefully. What point is it trying to make? What are the article's strengths? Weaknesses? Did the author of the article leave out something important? What do you have to say about the issue at hand? Do you have any new ideas? Identify one or two specific points that you would like to make about the issue in general and specifically about the published article you are writing about. Do not attempt to address every issue in the article you have selected, only one or two of the major ones.

How Do I Go About Writing the Letter?

Start by preparing an outline of the points you want to make in your letter (see Chapter 1). You should make no more than three major points, and one or two is better. You will, however, need to support your point(s) with persuasive argument, facts, and a clear explanation of the issue you are addressing. It is imperative to make your point clearly and immediately, and only then go on to defend it. It is a good practice, therefore, to have your thesis sentence (see Chapter 1, page 8) be the first sentence in the letter. Your thesis sentence is the main point you are trying to make. Either in or immediately after the thesis sentence, identify the article or editorial to which you are responding.

After your thesis sentence, present a concise, logical argument for the point you are making. Some other considerations are worthy of thought. Letters that sound too extreme are less likely to be effective than those that appear thoughtful and balanced. Be sure to write the letter so that it stands on its own, that is, the reader can understand it without having to read other materials. One more thing: Letters do not always have to be critical. It is often helpful to be as positive as possible, pointing out the competencies and successes of others.

The Importance of Correctness

Have you ever read something—an article, a billboard, an ad in the paper trying to convince you to take a particular action ("vote for me," "eat at Joe's") and found a glaring grammar error? "You're future is safe with Senator Smith." What does it do to your confidence in the argument being made to find that its writer is careless in this way? Most people find their attention going to the error, their focus deflected into rumination on the intelligence or education of the person who wrote or copied the offending text. It may not seem fair to you, but it's a fact: simple mistakes in your text can devastate your argument. In the case of a letter to the editor, a single typo or grammar error—"hat" instead of "has," "it's" instead of "its"—may be so off-putting to the editorial staff that your letter gets filed in the wastebasket rather than published. Proofread.

The format of your letter is important. You should use a standard business letter format. Most of them call for single spacing the text and the various addresses, double spacing only between paragraphs and between elements of the letter. In addition, look in the newspaper's editorial section and you will probably find specific directions and policies for submitting letters. Type your letter on good quality paper. Address the letter to the Editor. Include your name, address, phone number, and email address. The newspaper may check to be sure you are who you claim to be. After you write the letter, send it immediately so it will be fresh and pertinent. Check the paper daily to see if it has been printed. After a week, if you have not had a reply, send a follow-up letter to check your letter's status.

Sample Letter to the Editor

September 10, 2005

Mildred K. Feswick
Editor
Freetown Daily News
P.O, Box 2367
Freetown, TX 05672

Dear Ms. Feswick:

Education is the cornerstone of our society and deserves much more public support than it is currently getting. In an editorial that appeared on page 10 of the Freetown Daily News on Thursday, September 8, you stated "The Federal government spends too much money on education." I hope you will reconsider your opinion.

First, consider the impressive and pervasive value of education. The acquisition of knowledge is beneficial not only for the personal satisfaction that comes from learning about yourself and your culture, but for the resulting intellectual contributions to society as well. Statistics show that educated people make better decisions and contribute more to society than uneducated people do. National statistics clearly demonstrate the effectiveness of an education. College graduates have an unemployment rate that is half that of high school graduates, and the median income of a college graduate is $15,000 greater than the income of a high school graduate. Despite the effectiveness of these programs and the stunning statistics they produce, the government insists on cutting back on educational spending.

Parents are aware of the opportunities and insight a good education provides. In a recent poll, 98 percent of parents in America said they wanted their children to attend college. However, it is becoming increasingly difficult for parents to finance that education. Pell grants, which originally funded up to 75 percent of a student's education, now fund only up to 25 percent. Studies show that federal student aid programs have been extremely effective at educating people who otherwise could not have afforded college. Despite clear evidence that education is a good investment, it is not high on many legislators' lists of priorities. Funding for public schools and higher education is diminishing in the wake of excessive spending on other programs. For example, a report recently issued by the Justice Policy Institute, a research and advocacy organization in Washington, D.C., reveals that California and Florida now spend more money on prisons than on higher education. The report also says the average cost to incarcerate a felon is from $22,000 to $25,000 per year, the same amount charged by selective liberal arts colleges. If we can pay large sums of money to keep people from being productive, we should be able to find the funds to help people lead more productive and fulfilling lives.

President Bush has spearheaded the effort to slash educational appropriations programs. Rather than providing sufficient funds for public schools, his "No Child Left Behind" program withdraws funds from schools that do not meet federal standards. This policy might be reasonable if schools had adequate funding to begin with, but they don't. Many of the nation's teachers pay for school supplies out of their own pockets.

Education is the key to our country's economic future. We have the world's strongest economy because our educational institutions lead the world in producing competent graduates. It is therefore easy to see that the statement "The federal government spends too much money on education" is refuted by a thoughtful analysis of the benefits of federal aid to education. The comparatively small amount of money set aside for education is a clear indication of our country's lack of concern for our future. Today education is more important than ever. Our potential will go unmet unless we invest in properly training our minds. Education is the catalyst of a successful future.

Sincerely,

Jeremy M. Scott
3251 Matlock Road #22
Mansfield, TX 76063

10.2   OP-ED ESSAYS

An *op-ed essay* is a statement of perspective on an issue or matter of concern to the community that normally appears on the page of the newspaper "op-ed" (opposite the editorial page). It is neither an editorial (written by the newspaper editor) nor a letter to the editor (most often responding to an article or editorial previously published). Instead, it is a carefully formulated and engagingly written attention-grabbing essay that is intended primarily to stimulate thinking on part of newspaper readers with the ultimate goal of influencing their opinions. Unlike letters to the editor, an op-ed essay is often both an exercise in creative writing and a philosophical thought piece. Like letters to the editor, an op-ed's audience is the general public. Successful (published) op-ed essays usually display some or all of the following characteristics:

- A radical, incendiary, or at least distinctive point of view
- A new angle on a common topic
- A consistent, coherent theme
- Facts and anecdotes
- Humor or satire

How Do I Find a Topic?

Begin your topic search in the same manner you look for a topic for a letter to the editor. On the shelves of the periodicals room of your college library you will find the last several issues of your local newspaper. Read through them, looking for articles or other items that particularly interest you. Can you find something that you feel passionate about? Pay special attention to the op-ed pieces you find. Notice their subjects, styles, and approaches to issues. Pay special attention to their length. Find an issue that interests you personally and that you believe is of interest to people in your community. Identify one or two specific points that you would like to make about the issue.

How Do I Go About Writing the Op-ed Essay?

As you would with a letter to the editor, start by preparing an outline of the points you want to make in your essay (see Chapter 1). You should make no more than three major points in your essay. You will need to support your point(s) with persuasive argument, facts, and a clear explanation of the issue you are addressing. It is imperative to clearly and immediately make your point, and only then go on to defend it. It is a good practice, therefore, to make your thesis sentence the first sentence in the essay (see Chapter 1, page 8). Your thesis sentence is the main point you are trying to make.

After your thesis sentence, present a concise, logical argument for your point. Some other considerations are worthy of thought. Although op-ed pieces are often more radical in viewpoint than letters to the editor, an essay that simply thrashes at people or presents an unending stream of sarcasm is unlikely to be effective—or published. You may be dramatic to engage the reader, but be sure also to make a well-reasoned and well-documented argument. Be sure to write the essay so that it stands on its own, that is, so that the reader can understand it without reading other materials. Do not forget to proofread and check for spelling and grammar errors. As with letters to the editor, careful proofreading is absolutely essential to the success of your op-ed piece.

The format of your essay is important. You should format the essay as you would a college term paper (see Chapter 9). In addition, look in the newspaper's editorial section and you will probably find specific directions and policies for submitting op-ed essays. Type your essay on good quality paper. Include a cover letter to the editor citing your name, address, phone number, and email address. The newspaper may check to be sure you are who you claim to be. Check the paper daily to see if your essay has been printed. After a week, if you have not had a reply, send a follow-up letter to check your essay's status.

Sample Op-ed Essay

In her Christmas 2004 op-ed essay, *New York Times* columnist Maureen Dowd, the columnist conservatives love to hate, lambastes the Bush administration for its handling of the war in Iraq.

Christmas Eve of Destruction

By Maureen Dowd
New York Times, December 23, 2004

In Iraq, as Yogi Berra would say, the future ain't what it used to be.

Now that the election's over, our leaders think it's safe to experiment with a little candor.

President Bush has finally acknowledged that the Iraqis can't hack it as far as securing their own country, which means, of course, that America has no exit strategy for its troops, who will soon number 150,000.

News organizations led with the story, even though the president was only saying something that everybody has known to be true for a year. The White House's policy on Iraq has gone from a total charade to a limited modified hang-out. Mr. Bush is conceding the obvious, that the Iraqi security forces aren't perfect, so he doesn't have to concede the truth: that Iraq is now so dire no one knows how or when we can get out.

If this fiasco ever made sense to anybody, it doesn't any more.

John McCain, who lent his considerable credibility to Mr. Bush during the campaign and vouched for the president and his war, now concedes that he has no confidence in Donald Rumsfeld.

And Rummy admitted yesterday that his feelings got hurt when people accused him of being insensitive to the fact that he arrogantly sent his troops into a sinkhole of carnage—a vicious, persistent insurgency—without the proper armor, equipment, backup or preparation.

The subdued defense chief further admitted that despite all the American kids who gave their lives in Mosul on the cusp of Christmas, battling an enemy they can't see in a war fought over weapons that didn't exist, we're not heading toward the democratic halcyon Mr. Bush promised.

"I think looking for a peaceful Iraq after the elections would be a mistake," Mr. Rumsfeld said.

His disgraceful admission that his condolence letters to the families of soldiers killed in Iraq were signed by machine—"I have directed that in the future I sign each letter," he said in a Strangelovian statement—is redolent of the myopia that has led to the dystopia.

The Bushies are betting a lot on the January election, even though a Shiite-dominated government will further alienate the Sunnis—and even though Iraq may be run by an Iranian-influenced ayatollah. That would mean that Iraq would have a leadership legitimized by us to hate us.

International election observers say it's too dangerous to actually come in and monitor the vote in person; they're going to "assess" the vote from the safety of Amman, Jordan. Isn't that like refereeing a football game while sitting in a downtown bar?

The administration hopes that once the Iraqis understand they have their own government, that will be a turning point and they will realize their country is worth fighting for. But this is the latest in a long list of turning points that turn out to be cul-de-sacs.

From the capture of Saddam to the departure of Paul Bremer and the assault on Falluja, there have been many false horizons for peace.

The U.S. military can't even protect our troops when they're eating lunch in a supposedly secure space—even after the Mosul base commanders had been warned of a "Beirut-style" attack three weeks before—because the Iraqi security forces and support staff have been infiltrated by insurgency spies.

Each milestone, each thing that is supposed to enable us to get some traction and change the basic dynamic in Iraq, comes and goes without the security getting any better. The *Los Angeles Times* reported yesterday that a major U.S. contractor, Contrack International Inc., had dropped out of the multibillion-dollar effort to rebuild Iraq, "raising new worries about the country's growing violence and its effect on reconstruction."

The Bush crowd thought it could get in, get out, scare the Iranians and Syrians, and remove the bulk of our forces within several months.

But now we're in, and it's the allies, contractors and election watchdogs who want out.

Aside from his scintilla of candor, Mr. Bush is still not leveling with us. As he said at his press conference on Monday, "the enemies of freedom" know that "a democratic Iraq will be a decisive blow to their ambitions because free people will never choose to live in tyranny."

They may choose to live in a theocracy, though. Americans did.

New York Times, December 23, 2004 © *The New York Times.* Reprinted with permission.

10.3   LETTERS TO ELECTED REPRESENTATIVES

Elected representatives, especially members of the U.S. Senate and House of Representatives, receive scores of letters every day. Although you may write to wish your senator a happy birthday or complain about the senator's wardrobe, most letters to elected representatives are for two purposes: (1) to influence her or him to vote a certain way on an issue that is currently being considered before the legislature, or (2) to request that some member of the representative's staff perform a specific service, such as providing information or helping solve a problem encountered with a government agency. You may write a letter on any matter you please, but the goal of this particular assignment is to help you write the former type, that is, a letter that requests a representative to vote a certain way on impending legislation.

Letters to representatives are most likely to be influential when they are persuasively written and when they represent the view of a constituent. Your letter, therefore, should be addressed to your own senator or representative, and you should view it primarily as an exercise in persuasion. Letters that influence the votes of legislators often have several characteristics. First, they are brief and concise. Elected officials are very busy and, because they take in an immense amount of information each day, have very little patience for long-winded epistles that fail to get to the point. Second, good letters clearly identify a single action that the author wants the representative to take, stating and justifying the need for the requested action. Finally, good letters that concern a bill currently before Congress letter provide a brief summary of what the bill does. This may seem unnecessary, but Congress considers hundreds of bills each year, and often several appear simultaneously to address the same issue. You will want to save the representative some time by explaining exactly what she or he will be voting for.

How Do I Find a Topic?

The best place to start is THOMAS (http://thomas.loc.gov/), the home page of the Library of Congress, which provides online search engines and texts for all current legislation. Think of a topic in which you have a personal interest. Are you majoring in nursing? You may want to examine current legislation related to health care. Are you a music lover? Is any legislation passing that affects the music industry or your access to music on the Internet? Is there an issue pending that affects your personal congressional district? Whatever your interest, identify one or two key works and enter them into the THOMAS legislation search engine. You will then be presented a list of legislation in which your search terms are mentioned. After you locate a bill currently being considered by Congress that interests you, use the THOMAS Congressional Record search engine, enter the name of the bill, and you will find a record of speeches that have been made in Congress for and against the measure in question. Next, decide whether you are for or against the legislation and write down an initial list of your reasons for supporting or opposing it.

How Do I Go About Writing the Letter?

First, address your letter properly. A table providing proper forms of address is printed at the end of this section of this chapter. Begin your letter by telling the representative exactly what you want him or her to do and which piece of legislation is affected. Be sure to include the following information, which you will find when you locate the bill in the online *Congressional Digest:*

- Name of the bill (e.g., Environmental Justice Act of 2003)
- Subtitle of the bill (e.g., "an act to require Federal agencies to develop and implement policies and practices that promote environmental justice, and for other purposes")
- Bill's number (e.g., H. R. 2200)
- Current status of the bill (e.g., referred to the Subcommittee on Commercial and Administrative Law)

Next, address two of the legislator's primary concerns. For every bill that comes to the representative's attention, he or she must answer two questions: (1) "Is legislative action needed to deal with whatever problem or issue is at hand?" and (2) "If legislation is needed, is the specific legislation in question the best way to address the issue?" To answer these two questions you will need to make the following two arguments: (1) That the issue or problem warrants (or does not warrant) legislative action, and (2) that the specific proposed legislation appropriately deals (or does not appropriately deal) with the issue or problem.

Provide at least a few facts and examples or anecdotes. Include any personal experience or involvement that you have in the issue or problem. You do not need to provide all the information the legislator will need to make a decision, but provide enough to get her or him interested in the issue enough to examine the matter further and give it serious thought. Format the letter as you do a standard business letter and, of course, proofread your final draft carefully.

Sample Letter to a Representative

October 5, 2004

The Honorable Stephanie Herseth
1504 Longworth House Office Building
Washington, DC 20515

Dear Representative Herseth:

I am writing to ask you to vote for the Environmental Justice Act of 2003 (H. R. 2200, currently under consideration by the Subcommittee on Commercial and Administrative Law), an act "To require Federal agencies to develop and implement policies and practices that promote environmental justice, and for other purposes." Native Americans, Latinos, and Blacks have suffered too long under unhealthy environmental conditions on reservations and in substandard neighborhoods across the country. In my neighborhood the toxic waste from old mining operations has caused illness in more than twenty children.

Across the country Superfund sites and pockets of polluted air and water are affecting most the people with the fewest resources and the least political clout to deal with the problem. In Los Angeles, for example, more than seventy percent of African Americans and half of Latinos reside in the most highly polluted areas while only a third of the local whites live in these areas. Again, workers in the meatpacking plants of South Omaha, Nebraska, are battling to restore the vitality of city parks and improve unsanitary conditions in the plants. Too often people in these communities face greater exposure to toxins and dangerous substances because waste dumps, industrial facilities, and chemical storage facilities take fewer precautions in low income communities than they do in high income communities. Sadly, the captains of industry view these communities as expendable, denying the human beings who live in them the dignity and respect that is their constitutional right as American citizens.

What can be done? The first step is to solve a problem in and among federal agencies. Recent environmental and health policy studies have determined that most federal agencies, including the Environmental Protection Agency, do not adequately understand that environmental justice is being continuously denied to American citizens. Furthermore, there is currently no mechanism in place to coordinate and therefore make effective the environmental justice efforts that are currently under way.

The Environmental Justice Act of 2003 does much to correct these problems. In addition to focusing Federal agency attention on the environmental and human health conditions in minority, low-income, and Native American communities, this legislation takes several positive steps in the direction of securing environmental justice for Native Americans. It

- Ensures that all Federal agencies develop practices that promote environmental justice
- Increases cooperation and coordination among Federal agencies
- Provides minority, low-income, and Native American communities greater access to public information and opportunity for participation in environmental decision making
- Mitigates the inequitable distribution of the burdens and benefits of Federal programs having significant impact on human health and the environment, and
- Holds Federal agencies accountable for the effects of their projects and programs on all communities.

Your support in this urgent matter is much appreciated.

Sincerely,

P. Charles Longbranch III
18 Lake Charles Way
Passamadumcott, SD 57003

10.4 TABLE OF FORMS OF PROPER ADDRESS FORMATS

This table was adapted from Appendix 6 of the *Department of Defense Manual for Written Material* (March 2, 2004, Director of Administration and Management, Office of the Secretary of Defense). It provides proper address formats for a wide variety of elected and nonelected public officials at local, state, national, and international levels of government.

ADDRESSEE	ADDRESS ON LETTER AND ENVELOPE	SALUTATION AND CLOSE
The President	The President The White House 1600 Pennsylvania Avenue, NW Washington, DC 20500	Dear Mr./Madam President: Respectfully yours,
Spouse of the President	Mr./Mrs. (full name) The White House 1600 Pennsylvania Avenue, NW Washington, DC 20500	Dear Mr./Mrs. (surname): Sincerely,

ADDRESSEE	ADDRESS ON LETTER AND ENVELOPE	SALUTATION AND CLOSE
Director, Office of Management and Budget	The Honorable (full name) Director, Office of Management and Budget Washington, DC 20503	Dear Mr./Ms. (surname): Sincerely,
The Vice President	The Vice President 276 Eisenhower Executive Office Building Washington, DC 20501	Dear Mr./Madam Vice President: Sincerely,
The Chief Justice	The Chief Justice The Supreme Court Washington, DC 20543	Dear Chief Justice: Sincerely,
Associate Justice	The Honorable (full name) The Supreme Court Washington, DC 20543	Dear Justice (Surname): Sincerely,
Judge of a federal, state, or local court	The Honorable (full name) Judge of the (name of court) (address)	Dear Judge (surname): Sincerely,
Clerk of a court	Mr. (full name) Clerk of the (name of court) (address)	Dear Mr./Ms. (surname): Sincerely,
Senator (Washington office)	The Honorable (full name) United States Senate Washington, DC 20510-(+4 Code)	Dear Senator (surname): Sincerely,
Speaker of the House of Representatives	The Honorable (full name) Speaker of the House of Representatives U.S. House of Representatives Washington, DC 20515-(+4 Code)	Dear Mr./Madam Speaker: Sincerely,
Representative (Washington office)	The Honorable (full name) U.S. House of Representatives Washington, DC 20515-(+4 Code)	Dear Representative (surname): Sincerely,
Resident Commissioner	The Honorable (full name) Resident Commissioner from Puerto Rico U.S. House of Representatives Washington, DC 20515-(+4 Code)	Dear Mr./Ms. (surname): Sincerely,

(continued)

ADDRESSEE	ADDRESS ON LETTER AND ENVELOPE	SALUTATION AND CLOSE
Delegate	The Honorable (full name) Delegate from (location) U.S. House of Representatives Washington, DC 20515-(+4 Code)	Dear Mr./Ms. (surname): Sincerely,
Members of the Cabinet addressed as Secretary	The Honorable (full name) Secretary of (name of Department) Washington, DC (ZIP+4 Code)	Dear Mr./Madam Secretary: Sincerely,
Attorney General	The Honorable (full name) Attorney General Washington, DC 20530	Dear Mr. Attorney General: Sincerely,
Deputy Secretary of a department	The Honorable (full name) Deputy Secretary of (name of Department) Washington, DC (ZIP+4 Code)	Dear Mr./Ms. (surname): Sincerely,
Head of a federal agency, authority, or board	The Honorable (full name) (title) (agency) Washington, DC (ZIP+4 Code)	Dear Mr./Ms. (surname): Sincerely,
President of a commission or board	The Honorable (full name) President, (name of commission) Washington, DC (ZIP+4 Code)	Dear Mr./Ms. (surname): Sincerely,
Chairman of a commission or board	The Honorable (full name) Chairman, (name of commission) Washington, DC (ZIP+4 Code)	Dear Mr./Madam Chairman: Sincerely,
Postmaster General	The Honorable (full name) Postmaster General 475 L'Enfant Plaza West, SW Washington, DC 20260	Dear Mr./Madam Postmaster General: Sincerely,
American Ambassador	The Honorable (full name) American Ambassador(city) (city), (country)	Dear Mr./Madam Ambassador: Sincerely,
Foreign ambassador in the United States	His/Her Excellency (full name) Ambassador of (country) Washington, DC (ZIP+4 Code)	Dear Mr./Madam Ambassador: Sincerely,
Secretary General of the United Nations	The Honorable (full name) Secretary General of the United Nations New York, NY 10017	Dear Mr./Madam Secretary General: Sincerely,

ADDRESSEE	ADDRESS ON LETTER AND ENVELOPE	SALUTATION AND CLOSE
United States Representative to the United Nations	The Honorable (full name) United States Representative to the United Nations New York, NY 10017	Dear Mr./Ms. (surname): Sincerely,
State Governor	The Honorable (full name) Governor of (state) (city), (state) (ZIP Code)	Dear Governor (surname): Sincerely,
State Lieutenant Governor	The Honorable (full name) Lieutenant Governor of (state) (city), (state) (ZIP Code)	Dear Mr./Ms. (surname): Sincerely,
State Secretary of State	The Honorable (full name) Secretary of State of (state) (city), (state) (ZIP Code)	Dear Mr./Madam (surname): Sincerely,
Chief Justice of a State Supreme Court	The Honorable (full name) Chief Justice Supreme Court of the State of (state) (city), (state) (ZIP Code)	Dear Mr./Madam Chief Justice: Sincerely,
State Attorney General	The Honorable (full name) Attorney General State of (state) (city), (state) (ZIP Code)	Dear Mr./Madam Attorney General: Sincerely,
State Treasurer, Comptroller, or Auditor	The Honorable (full name) State Treasurer (Comptroller) (Auditor) State of (state) (city), (state) (ZIP Code)	Dear Mr./Ms. (surname): Sincerely,
President, State Senate	The Honorable (full name) President of the Senate of the State of (state) (city), (state) (ZIP Code)	Dear Mr./Ms. (surname): Sincerely,
State Senator	The Honorable (full name) (state) Senate (city), (state) (ZIP Code)	Dear Mr./Ms. (surname): Sincerely,
Speaker, State House of Representatives, Assembly or House of Delegates	The Honorable (full name) Speaker of the House of Representatives (Assembly) (House of Delegates) of the State of (state) (city), (state) (ZIP Code)	Dear Mr./Ms. (surname): Sincerely,

(continued)

ADDRESSEE	ADDRESS ON LETTER AND ENVELOPE	SALUTATION AND CLOSE
State Representative, Assemblyman, or Delegate	The Honorable (full name) (state) House of Representatives (Assembly) (House of Delegates) (city), (state) (ZIP Code)	Dear Mr./Ms. (surname): Sincerely,
Mayor	The Honorable (full name) Mayor of (city) (city), (state) (ZIP Code)	Dear Mayor (surname) Sincerely,
President of a Board of Commissioners	The Honorable (full name) President, Board of Commissioners of (city) (city), (state) (ZIP Code)	Dear Mr./Ms. (surname): Sincerely,

◆ CHAPTER 11 ◆
Critical Thinking Exercises

As you have probably already discovered, college, among other things it does, helps you increase your knowledge, develop your communications skills, and clarify your fundamental values. The following exercises provide a means of attaining these three objectives simultaneously. Writing these essays will help you learn to (1) observe critically, (2) grasp the political power of metaphor, (3) clarify your fundamental values, and (4) improve your ability to explain your thoughts to others.

11.1   AN INTRODUCTION TO THE OBSERVATION OF POLITICS

Using simple questionnaires, psychologists can easily demonstrate that few people recall with any detail or accuracy events that happened just moments before the questionnaires were distributed. Considerable evidence suggests that many of us go through our lives from one day to the next observing virtually nothing at all. Perhaps we can do better.

Successful scientists agree that precise, prolonged, detailed observation initiates discovery. Greek philosopher Aristotle (384–322 BCE), German physicist Albert Einstein (1879–1955), and French psychologist Jean Piaget (1896–1980) permanently altered how we see the world. Surprisingly, they did so neither by accidentally stumbling upon hidden mystical phenomena nor by activating rational processes available only to geniuses. Instead, they all did it the simplest (and perhaps the hardest) way possible. They simply looked at what was directly in front of them—in front of each of us—in everyday life. They did so, however, with much more patience, intensity, and precision that we are normally willing to use.

Einstein is a clear example. He revolutionized his generation's concepts of time and matter, the very substance of the universe. He also taught us that the ordinary is the key to the extraordinary. As a young adult Einstein worked as a clerk at a patent office in Geneva, Switzerland. On the train to and from work, instead of reading the newspaper, Einstein stared out the window, gazing for many hours at the appearance of telegraph poles passing through the passenger car windows. For a period of two weeks he spent his evening hours at home staring at tea leaves as they floated to the bottom of his cup. Over and over, hour after hour, day after day, he stirred them, just to watch the movements they made as they fell to the bottom of the cup. Had we been able to observe Einstein during these moments, we would likely conclude that his mental capacities were abnormal or deficient. But the long hours he spent observing such common processes led him to insights that changed life as we know it.

Jean Piaget thought and acted like Einstein. A founding father of developmental psychology, a person who restructured our way of understanding how children work, play, interact, and become adults, Piaget formulated his theories after spending many months, one day at a time, sitting in a school yard with his notebooks, patiently writing down everything he saw and heard. Billions of mothers may have loved their children, but not one of them, as far as we know, saw their children as clearly as Piaget saw the subjects of his schoolyard observations.

Aristotle, who preceded Einstein and Piaget by more than two millennia, became known as the father of political science when he applied what is now known as the scientific method to the study of politics. His mentor Plato had studied politics by applying deductive reasoning to problems of justice and good government. Aristotle, to the contrary, in order to understand what good government is, decided to look not to pure rationality but instead to consider governments existing in the world around him. The very first words of Aristotle's monumental *Politics* are "Observation shows us. . . ." He successfully examined and categorized more than 350 of the city-states of the Mediterranean world of his day, and political scientists have been following his example ever since.

11.2   DIRECTIONS FOR AN EXERCISE IN OBSERVATION: CAMPAIGN COMMERCIALS

Now it is your turn to observe politics. Using the directions that follow, and employing the paper formats described in previous chapters in this book, write a ten-page (double-spaced) paper.

1. On the Internet locate this Web site: http://livingroomcandidate. movingimage. us/index.php Here you will find a collection of televised presidential campaign commercials from 1952 to 2004.
2. Browsing through the offerings, view several commercials in different years in order to familiarize yourself with the variety of campaign ads offered.
3. Select six commercials, no more than two from any one candidate.
4. Make a set of notes for yourself (not to be submitted to the instructor) that answer at least the following questions for each of the six commercials:
   a. Which party has prepared the commercial?
   b. Who is portrayed in the commercial?

    c. What, exactly, does the commercial say?

    d. What "techniques," such as humor, sarcasm, irony, fear, education, or slander, does the commercial use to get its point across?

    e. What is the specific objective (beyond getting a particular candidate elected) of this particular commercial?

    f. What is the commercial attempting to imply about the candidates involved in that particular race?

    g. What is the commercial attempting to imply about an issue or issues involved in that particular race?

    h. To what extent is the message of the commercial "positive," that is, portraying someone or some idea in an optimistic or affirming way?

    i. To what extent is the message of the commercial "negative," that is, portraying someone or some idea in a disapproving or unenthusiastic way?

    j. How accurate is the commercial?

    k. How honest is the commercial?

    l. How effective is the commercial?

    m. What criteria have you used to assess the effectiveness of the commercial?

    n. What does this commercial tell you about the candidate who sponsored it?

    o. What does this commercial tell you about the candidate at whom the commercial is aimed?

    p. What does this commercial tell you about American politics?

5. Now, using your observations generated by answering the questions above, write a ten-page essay in which you evaluate and compare the commercials you have viewed. In the course of your essay,

- Describe the six commercials (election year, sponsoring candidate, commercial content)
- Compare the techniques used
- Compare the effectiveness of the commercials
- Explain what this exercise in observation has showed you about American politics

11.3 DIRECTIONS FOR WRITING AN ALLEGORY ANALYSIS

Webster's New Collegiate Dictionary defines *allegory* as "the expression by means of symbolic fictional figures and actions of truths or generalizations about human existence . . . an instance (as in a story or painting) of such expression . . . a symbolic representation." An allegory often appears in the form of a *parable* (*Webster:* a "short fictitious story that illustrates a moral attitude or a religious principle").

Most of us are introduced to allegories before we have the slightest understanding of what they mean. Our parents often begin reading us their favorite fables and children's stories—the "Three Little Pigs," "Goldilocks and the Three Bears," "Little Red Riding Hood"—long before we are able to read them or apply them to our lives.

Successful philosophers (intuitive observers all) appreciate allegory as a tool for helping the human mind grasp the meaning of what it has observed. Aristotle's mentor Plato, Harvard University political scientist John Rawls, and French philosopher Michel Foucault have provided powerful allegories, summarized below, that offer us the opportunity not only to understand the political world better, but to clarify some of our own fundamental values as well.

Complete the following tasks in writing your political allegory analysis paper. First, read the political allegories and the "matters for consideration" following each allegory provided in the next three sections of this chapter (Sections 11.4, 11.5, and 11.6). Second, select one of the allegories as the focus of your analysis. Third, write a five- to seven-page essay about the selected allegory in which you:

1. Summarize the allegory
2. Identify precisely the meaning the author is attempting to convey
3. Explain the implications of the allegory
4. Apply the symbolic meaning of the allegory to politics in America or the world today
5. Utilize the "matters for consideration" provided after each allegory without limiting yourself exclusively to them

11.4   ALLEGORY 1: PLATO'S RING OF GYGES

Plato (427–347 BCE), father of political philosophy, recorded his mentor Socrates' most influential ideas in the form of fictional dialogues, conversations that Socrates held with prominent Athenians of his day. Although many of the dialogues address political issues, Plato's most important treatise on politics is contained in *The Republic,* in which Socrates discusses justice and how it is to be achieved in society. In Book II of *The Republic* Glaucon, one of Socrates' imaginary interlocutors, insists that to be just—that is, to follow commonly accepted standards of justice—is rational only if one is constrained to do so:

> They say that to do injustice is, by nature, good; to suffer injustice, evil; but that the evil is greater than the good. And so when men have both done and suffered injustice and have had experience of both, not being able to avoid the one and obtain the other, they think that they had better agree among themselves to have neither; hence there arise laws and mutual covenants; and that which is ordained by law is termed by them lawful and just. This they affirm to be the origin and nature of justice;—it is a mean or compromise, between the best of all, which is to do injustice and not be punished, and the worst of all, which is to suffer injustice without the power of retaliation; and justice, being at a middle point between the two, is tolerated not as a good, but as the lesser evil, and honoured by reason of the inability of men to do injustice. For no man who is worthy to be called a man would ever submit to such an agreement if he were able to resist; he would be mad if he did. Such is the received account, Socrates, of the nature and origin of justice.

Now that those who practise justice do so involuntarily and because they have not the power to be unjust will best appear if we imagine something of this kind: having given both to the just and the unjust power to do what they will, let us watch and see whither desire will lead them; then we shall discover in the very act the just and unjust man to be proceeding along the same road, following their interest, which all natures deem to be their good, and are only diverted into the path of justice by the force of law. The liberty which we are supposing may be most completely given to them in the form of such a power as is said to have been possessed by Gyges the ancestor of Croesus the Lydian. According to the tradition, Gyges was a shepherd in the service of the king of Lydia; there was a great storm, and an earthquake made an opening in the earth at the place where he was feeding his flock. Amazed at the sight, he descended into the opening, where, among other marvels, he beheld a hollow brazen horse, having doors, at which he stooping and looking in saw a dead body of stature, as appeared to him, more than human, and having nothing on but a gold ring; this he took from the finger of the dead and reascended. Now the shepherds met together, according to custom, that they might send their monthly report about the flocks to the king; into their assembly he came having the ring on his finger, and as he was sitting among them he chanced to turn the collet of the ring inside his hand, when instantly he became invisible to the rest of the company and they began to speak of him as if he were no longer present. He was astonished at this, and again touching the ring he turned the collet outwards and reappeared; he made several trials of the ring, and always with the same result—when he turned the collet inwards he became invisible, when outwards he reappeared. Whereupon he contrived to be chosen one of the messengers who were sent to the court; where as soon as he arrived he seduced the queen, and with her help conspired against the king and slew him, and took the kingdom. Suppose now that there were two such magic rings, and the just put on one of them and the unjust the other; no man can be imagined to be of such an iron nature that he would stand fast in justice. No man would keep his hands off what was not his own when he could safely take what he liked out of the market, or go into houses and lie with any one at his pleasure, or kill or release from prison whom he would, and in all respects be like a God among men. Then the actions of the just would be as the actions of the unjust; they would both come at last to the same point. And this we may truly affirm to be a great proof that a man is just, not willingly or because he thinks that justice is any good to him individually, but of necessity, for wherever any one thinks that he can safely be unjust, there he is unjust. For all men believe in their hearts that injustice is far more profitable to the individual than justice, and he who argues as I have been supposing, will say that they are right. If you could imagine any one obtaining this power of becoming invisible, and never doing any wrong or touching what was another's, he would be thought by the lookers-on to be a most wretched idiot, although they would praise him to one another's faces, and keep up appearances with one another from a fear that they too might suffer injustice. Enough of this. (Jowett http://classics.mit.edu/Plato/republic.3.ii.html)

Matters for Consideration

1. What would you do if you had Gyges' ring?
2. To what extent are people naturally unjust?

3. To what extent are people constrained from injustice only by fear of penalty?
4. If Glaucon is right, how should society be constructed?
5. If Glaucon is wrong, how should society be constructed?

11.5   ALLEGORY 2: RAWLS' VEIL OF IGNORANCE

The late Harvard University political scientist John Rawls (1921–2002) reinvigorated the ancient quest for justice and good government in his works, the most prominent of which is *A Theory of Justice*. In this book Rawls proposes a particular set of definitions of justice, equality, and freedom. Of interest for this writing exercise is an allegory Rawls employs to answer the question Socrates pursued in *The Republic:* "What is justice?" Rawls replies: "Justice is fairness."

Rawls proposes, in part, that to understand how justice as fairness can be actualized in society we must imagine ourselves to be participant in an allegory that may be called the "veil of ignorance." First we assume an "original position of equality."

> In justice as fairness the original position of equality corresponds to the state of nature in the traditional theory of the social contract. This original position is not, of course, thought of as an actual historical state of affairs, much less as a primitive condition of culture. It is understood as a purely hypothetical situation characterized so as to lead to a certain conception of justice. Among the essential features of this situation is that no one knows his place in society, his class position or social status, nor does any one know his fortune in the distribution of natural assets and abilities, his intelligence, strength, and the like. I shall even assume that the parties do not know their conceptions of the good or their special psychological propensities. The principles of justice are chosen behind a veil of ignorance (Rawls 12).

Just to make sure we understand what Rawls is getting at here, let's paraphrase, very liberally, using a common religious metaphor that Rawls does not use. Imagine you are up in heaven standing in line waiting to be born. Like the other souls before and after you, you enter the next conceived fetus, wherever it occurs on earth. You have no idea whether you will be born in Massachusetts, the Ukraine, or the Congo. You have no idea whether your mother will be a Hollywood star or a drug-addicted prostitute. You have no idea whether your father will be a multimillionaire or a slave in the Sudan. You have no idea if your IQ will be 150 or 50, whether you will have the physique of Arnold Schwarzeneggar or the functional capacities of a quadriplegic, or if you will physically resemble Tom Cruise or Quasimodo. While you are pondering the odds, the archangel Michael tells you and the other prenatal souls that you have been granted the chance to construct the constitution of the society in which you will live.

Matters for Consideration

1. What specific constitutional measures will you propose in order to construct a society that will protect your interest should you be someone who is physically or mentally disadvantaged?
2. What specific constitutional measures will you propose in order to construct a society that will protect your interest should you be someone who is financially disadvantaged?
3. What specific constitutional measures will you propose in order to construct a society that will protect your interest should you be someone who is physically or mentally superior?
4. What specific constitutional measures will you propose in order to construct a society that will protect your interest should you be someone who is financially advantaged?
5. What specific constitutional measures will you propose in order to construct a society that will protect the interests of everyone in the categories listed immediately above?

11.6   ALLEGORY 3: FOUCAULT'S PANOPTICON

French philosopher Michel Foucault (1926–1984) wrote several volumes of what he called genealogy. He was not interested in tracing family trees. Instead, he attempted to trace patterns of political power as they emerged in society. He was most interested in identifying how political power is created and wielded and how people perceive it and are affected by it. His studies led him to conclude that political power is much more pervasive than many people assume. To illustrate his principle he proposed an allegorical panopticon.

A real, tangible panopticon had been invented by the eighteenth-century British utilitarian philosopher Jeremy Bentham. Bentham wanted to reform the British penal system. As Foucault notes in *Discipline and Punish* (1991), in 1791 Bentham proposed a new, more humane, and more efficient prison design than was in use in the eighteenth and nineteenth centuries:

> Bentham's Panopticon is the architectural figure of this composition. We know the principle on which it was based: at the periphery, an annular building; at the centre, a tower; this tower is pierced with wide windows that open onto the inner side of the ring; the peripheric building is divided into cells, each of which extends the whole width of the building; they have two windows, one on the inside, corresponding to the windows of the tower; the other, on the outside, allows the light to cross the cell from one end to the other. All that is needed, then, is to place a supervisor in a central tower and to shut up in each cell a madman, a patient, a condemned man, a worker or a schoolboy. By the effect of backlighting, one can observe from the tower, standing out precisely against the light, the small captive shadows in the cells of the periphery. They are like so many cages, so many small theatres, in which each actor is alone, perfectly individualized and constantly visible.

The panoptic mechanism arranges spatial unities that make it possible to see constantly and to recognize immediately. In short, it reverses the principle of the dungeon; or rather of its three functions—to enclose, to deprive of light and to hide—it preserves only the first and eliminates the other two. Full lighting and the eye of a supervisor capture better than darkness, which ultimately protected. Visibility is a trap.

To begin with, this made it possible—as a negative effect—to avoid those compact, swarming, howling masses that were to be found in places of confinement, those painted by Goya or described by Howard. Each individual, in his place, is securely confined to a cell from which he is seen from the front by the supervisor; but the side walls prevent him from coming into contact with his companions. He is seen, but he does not see; he is the object of information, never a subject in communication. The arrangement of his room, opposite the central tower, imposes on him an axial visibility; but the divisions of the ring, those separated cells, imply a lateral invisibility. And this invisibility is a guarantee of order. If the inmates are convicts, there is no danger of a plot, an attempt at collective escape, the planning of new crimes for the future, bad reciprocal influences; if they are patients, there is no danger of contagion; if they are madmen there is no risk of their committing violence upon one another; if they are schoolchildren, there is no copying, no noise, no chatter, no waste of time; if they are workers, there are no disorders, no theft, no coalitions, none of those distractions that slow down the rate of work, make it less perfect or cause accidents. The crowd, a compact mass, a locus of multiple exchanges, individualities merging together, a collective effect, is abolished and replaced by a collection of separated individualities. From the point of view of the guardian, it is replaced by a multiplicity that can be numbered and supervised; from the point of view of the inmates, by a sequestered and observed solitude [Bentham, 60–64].

Hence the major effect of the Panopticon: to induce in the inmate a state of conscious and permanent visibility that assures the automatic functioning of power. So to arrange things that the surveillance is permanent in its effects, even if it is discontinuous in its action; that the perfection of power should tend to render its actual exercise unnecessary; that this architectural apparatus should be a machine for creating and sustaining a power relation independent of the person who exercises it; in short, that the inmates should be caught up in a power situation of which they are themselves the bearers. To achieve this, it is at once too much and too little that the prisoner should be constantly observed by an inspector: too little, for what matters is that he knows himself to be observed; too much, because he has no need in fact of being so. In view of this, Bentham laid down the principle that power should be visible and unverifiable. Visible: the inmate will constantly have before his eyes the tall outline of the central tower from which he is spied upon. Unverifiable: the inmate must never know whether he is being looked at at any one moment; but he must be sure that he may always be so. In order to make the presence or absence of the inspector unverifiable, so that the prisoners, in their cells, cannot even see a shadow, Bentham envisaged not only venetian blinds on the windows of the central observation hall, but, on the inside, partitions that intersected the hall at right angles and, in order to pass from one quarter to the other, not doors but zig-zag openings; for the slightest noise, a gleam of light, a brightness in a half-opened door would betray the presence of the guardian. The Panopticon is a machine for dissociating the see/being seen dyad: in the peripheric ring, one is totally seen, without ever seeing; in the central tower, one sees everything without ever being seen.

It is an important mechanism, for it automatizes and disindividualizes power. Power has its principle not so much in a person as in a certain concerted distribution of bodies, surfaces, lights, gazes; in an arrangement whose internal mechanisms produce the relation in which individuals are caught up. The ceremonies, the rituals, the marks by which the sovereign's surplus power was manifested are useless. There is a machinery that assures dissymmetry, disequilibrium, difference. Consequently, it does not matter who exercises power. Any individual, taken almost at random, can operate the machine: in the absence of the director, his family, his friends, his visitors, even his servants (Bentham, 45). Similarly, it does not matter what motive animates him: the curiosity of the indiscreet, the malice of a child, the thirst for knowledge of a philosopher who wishes to visit this museum of human nature, or the perversity of those who take pleasure in spying and punishing. The more numerous those anonymous and temporary observers are, the greater the risk for the inmate of being surprised and the greater his anxious awareness of being observed. The Panopticon is a marvellous machine which, whatever use one may wish to put it to, produces homogeneous effects of power.

A real subjection is born mechanically from a fictitious relation. So it is not necessary to use force to constrain the convict to good behaviour, the madman to calm, the worker to work, the schoolboy to application, the patient to the observation of the regulations. Bentham was surprised that panoptic institutions could be so light: there were no more bars, no more chains, no more heavy locks; all that was needed was that the separations should be clear and the openings well arranged. The heaviness of the old "houses of security," with their fortress-like architecture, could be replaced by the simple, economic geometry of a "house of certainty." The efficiency of power, its constraining force, have, in a sense, passed over to the other side—to the side of its surface of application. He who is subjected to a field of visibility, and who knows it, assumes responsibility for the constraints of power; he makes them play spontaneously upon himself; he inscribes in himself the power relation in which he simultaneously plays both roles; he becomes the principle of his own subjection. By this very fact, the external power may throw off its physical weight; it tends to the non-corporal; and, the more it approaches this limit, the more constant, profound and permanent are its effects: it is a perpetual victory that avoids any physical confrontation and which is always decided in advance.(Foucault [1995], 195–228)

Matters for Consideration

1. Foucault's allegorical Panopticon, unlike Bentham's actual panopticon, is not a prison, but society itself.
2. To what extent are we, as members of society, inmates of a panopticon?
3. To what extent are we, as members of society, guards in a panopticon?
4. Although we are members of a "free" society, how much freedom do we actually have to express our individuality?
5. What can be done to enhance our freedom to express our individuality?

◆ CHAPTER 12 ◆
Policy Analysis Papers

12.1   THE BASICS OF POLICY ANALYSIS

What Is Policy Analysis?

Policy analysis is the examination of the components of a decision in order to enable one to act according to a set principle or rule in a given set of circumstances (a policy). This analysis is conducted at the local, state, national, and international levels of government. The most publicized reports tend, naturally, to be those of presidential commissions. Presidents create commissions to do policy analysis. This means that the president appoints a group of people to study possible government policies on a certain topic or problem, and report their findings and recommendations.

Policy Analysis in Action: The Brownlow Commission Report (1937)

Numerous presidential commissions have studied a wide range of subjects, including crime, poverty, and violence. One of the most famous, and one that had far-reaching effects, was the President's Committee on Administrative Management of 1937, known as the Brownlow Commission for one of its three primary authors, Louis Brownlow.

President Roosevelt appointed the Brownlow Commission to find ways to make the operation of the bureaucracy more efficient. The commission found "in the American government at the present time that the effectiveness of the chief executive is limited and restricted; . . . that the work of the executive branch is badly organized; that the managerial agencies are weak and out of date." In response to these problems, the commission made the following five recommendations to the president:

1. To deal with the greatly increased duties of executive management falling on the president, the White House staff should be expanded.

2. The managerial agencies of the government, particularly those dealing with the budget, efficiency research, personnel, and planning, should be greatly strengthened and developed as arms of the chief executive.

3. The merit system should be extended upward, outward, and downward to cover all nonpolicy-determining posts; the civil service system should be reorganized; and opportunities established for a career system attractive to the best talent in the nation.

4. The whole executive branch of the government should be overhauled and the present 100 agencies reorganized under a few large departments in which every executive activity would find its place.

5. The fiscal system should be extensively revised in light of the best governmental and private practice, particularly with reference to financial records, audit, and accountability of the executive to Congress. (President's Committee 1937, 4)

12.2   PRELUDE TO POLICY ANALYSIS: POLICY ANALYSIS RESEARCH PROPOSALS

This chapter includes directions for two types of paper assignments: a policy analysis research *proposal* and a policy analysis research *paper*. The proposal is a description of the research that will be conducted during the writing of the research paper. This assignment is included here because students who hope to become policy analysts will find that, when working in or consulting to government organizations, they will almost always be required to submit a proposal explaining and justifying the research that they expect to do before they are commissioned or funded to conduct the research itself.

The Purpose of Research Proposals

Research proposals are sales jobs. Their purpose is to "sell" the belief that a research study needs to be done. As part of this "selling" process, you will have to submit a policy analysis research proposal designed to accomplish the following seven tasks:

1. Prove that the study is necessary.
2. Describe the objectives of the study.
3. Explain how the study will be done.
4. Describe the resources (time, people, equipment, facilities, etc.) that will be needed to do the job.
5. Construct a schedule that states when the project will begin and end, and gives important dates in between.
6. Prepare a project budget that specifies the financial costs and the amount to be billed (if any) to the government agency.
7. Carefully define what the research project will produce, what kind of study will be conducted, how long it will be, and what it will contain.

The Content of Research Proposals

An Overview

In form, policy analysis research proposals contain the following four parts:

1. Title page (You may follow the format prescribed by your instructor or institution, or use the format shown in Chapter 3.)
2. Outline page (This is very important and must be done correctly. For directions and an example, see Chapter 3.)
3. Text
4. Reference page

An outline of the content of policy analysis proposals appears below:

I. Need for a policy analysis study
  A. An initial description of the current policy problem
    1. A definition of the deficiency in or problem with the current policy
    2. A brief history of the policy problem
    3. The legal framework and institutional setting of the policy problem
    4. The character of the policy problem, including its size, extent, and importance
  B. Policy analysis imperatives
II. Objectives of the proposed policy analysis study
  A. Clarification of the current policy problem
    1. A better problem definition
    2. A better estimate of the quality and quantity of the problem
    3. A more accurate projection of policy problem development
  B. An accurate evaluation of current relevant public policy
    1. An evaluation of the primary current applicable public policy
      a. A clarification of the primary policy
      b. A clarification of the legal foundation of the primary policy
      c. A clarification of the historical development of the policy
      d. A clarification of the environment of the policy
      e. A description of current policy implementation
      f. An evaluation of the effectiveness and efficiency of the policy
    2. An evaluation of secondary applicable public policies
  C. An evaluation of alternatives to present policies
    1. A presentation of possible alternative policies
    2. A comparative evaluation of the expected costs and benefits of the present and alternative policies
III. Methodology of the proposed policy analysis study
  A. Project management methods to be used
  B. Research methods to be used
  C. Data analysis methods to be used
IV. Resources necessary to conduct the study
  A. Material resources
  B. Human resources
  C. Financial resources

12.3   POLICY ANALYSIS PAPERS

Definition: A Policy Analysis Paper

A policy analysis paper evaluates a decision by reviewing current and potential government policies. It is a document written to help decision makers select the best policy for solving a particular problem. In writing a policy analysis paper, you should:

1. Select and clearly define a specific government policy
2. Carefully define the social, governmental, economic, or other problem the policy is designed to solve
3. Describe the economic, social, and political environments in which the problem arose and in which the existing policy for solving the problem was developed
4. Evaluate the effectiveness of the current policy or lack of policy in dealing with the problem
5. Identify alternative policies that could be adopted to solve the selected problem, and estimate the economic, social, environmental, and political costs and benefits of each alternative
6. Provide a summary comparison of all policies examined

Policy analysis papers are written every day at all levels of government. Public officials are constantly challenged to initiate new policies or change old ones. If they have a current formal policy at all, they want to know how effective it is. They then want to know what options are available to them, what changes they might make to improve current policy, and what the consequences of those changes will be. Policies are reviewed under a number of circumstances. Policy analyses are sometimes conducted as part of the normal agency budgeting processes. They help decision makers decide what policies should be continued or discontinued. They may be very narrow in scope, such as deciding the hours of operation of facilities at city parks. Or they may be very broad, such as deciding how the nation will provide health care or defense for its citizens.

The Purpose of Policy Analysis Papers

Successful policy analysis papers all share the same general purpose: to inform policy makers about how public policy in a specific area may be improved.

Elected officials are employed full-time in the business of making public policy. Legislators at the state and national levels hire staff people who continually investigate public policy issues and seek ways to improve legislated policy. At the national level, the Congressional Research Service continually finds information for representatives and senators. Each committee of Congress employs staff members who help it review current laws and define options for making new ones. State legislatures also employ their own research agencies and committee staff. Legislators and other policy makers are also given policy information by hundreds of public interest groups and research organizations.

A policy analysis paper, like a position paper, is an entirely practical exercise. It is neither theoretical nor general. Its objective is to identify and evaluate the policy options that are available for a specific topic.

The Contents of a Policy Analysis Paper

Summary of the Contents

Policy analysis papers contain six basic elements:

1. Title page
2. Executive summary
3. Table of contents, including a list of tables and illustrations
4. Text (or body)
5. References to sources of information
6. Appendixes

Parameters of the Text

Ask your instructor for the number of pages required for the policy analysis paper assigned for your course. Such papers at the undergraduate level often range from twenty to fifty pages (double-spaced, typed) in length.

Two general rules govern the amount of information presented in the body of the paper. First, content must be adequate to make a good policy evaluation. All the facts necessary to understand the significant strengths and weaknesses of a policy and its alternatives must be included. If your paper omits a fact that is critical to the decision, a poor decision will likely be made.

Never omit important facts merely because they tend to support a perspective other than your own. It is your responsibility to present the facts as clearly as possible, not to bias the evaluation in a particular direction.

The second guideline for determining the length of a policy analysis paper is to omit extraneous material. Include only the information that is helpful in making the particular decision at hand.

The Format of a Policy Analysis Paper

Title Page

The title page for a policy analysis paper should follow the format provided in Chapter 3.

Executive Summary

A one-page, single-spaced executive summary immediately follows the title page. An executive summary is composed of carefully written sentences expressing the central concepts that are more fully explained in the text of the paper. The purpose of the summary is to allow the decision maker to understand, as quickly as possible, the major considerations to be discussed. Each statement must be clearly defined and carefully prepared. The decision maker should be able to get a clear and thorough overview of the entire policy problem and the value and costs of available policy options by reading nothing but the one-page summary.

Table of Contents

The table of contents of a policy analysis paper must follow the organization of the paper's text and should conform to the format shown in Chapter 3.

Text

A policy analysis paper should follow the outline shown below:

I. Description of the policy currently in force
    A. A clear, concise statement of the policy currently in force
    B. A brief history of the policy currently in force
    C. A description of the problem the current policy was aimed at resolving, including an estimate of its extent and importance
II. Environments of the policy currently in force
    A. A description of the social and physical factors affecting the origin, development, and implementation of the current policy
    B. A description of the economic factors affecting the origin, development, and implementation of the current policy
    C. A description of the political factors affecting the origin, development, and implementation of the current policy
III. Effectiveness and efficiency of the current policy
    A. How well the existing policy does what it was designed to do
    B. How well the policy performs in relation to the effort and resources committed to it
IV. Policy alternatives
    A. Possible alterations of the present policy, with the estimated costs and benefits of each
    B. Alternatives to the present policy, with the estimated costs and benefits of each
V. Summary comparison of policy options

Each of the policy analysis components listed in the outline above is described in detail in most public policy analysis text books. Be sure to discuss the outline with your instructor to make ensure that you understand what each entails.

References

All sources of information in a policy analysis paper must be properly cited, following the directions in Chapter 4.

Appendixes

Appendixes can provide the reader of policy analysis papers with information that supplements the important facts contained in the text. For many local development and public works projects, a map and a diagram are often very helpful appendixes. You should attach them to the end of the paper, after the reference page. You should not append entire government reports, journal articles, or other publications, but selected charts, graphs, or other pages may be included. The source of the information should always be evident on the appended pages.

◆ CHAPTER 13 ◆
Amicus Curiae Briefs

13.1 HOW TO WRITE AMICUS CURIAE BRIEFS FOR THE UNITED STATES SUPREME COURT

When people are parties to disputes before the United States Supreme Court, the attorneys representing each side prepare written documents called *briefs on the merit*, which explain the nature of the dispute and present an argument for the side the attorney represents. The justices read the briefs, hear oral arguments, hold conferences to discuss the case, and then write opinions to announce both the Court's decision and the views of justices who disagree in whole or in part with that decision. Cases that come before the Supreme Court are usually important to many people who are not actually parties to the specific case being presented, because the Court's decisions contain principles and guidelines that all lower courts must follow in deciding similar cases. *Roe v. Wade*, for example, did not become famous because it allowed one person to have an abortion free from the constraints of the laws of Texas, but because it set forth the principle that state law may not restrict abortions in the first three months of pregnancy to protect the fetus.

Because Supreme Court cases are important to people other than those directly involved in the case, sometimes groups and individuals outside the proceedings of a specific case want their views on cases to be heard by the Court before it makes a decision. It is not proper, however, to go to the justices directly and try to influence them to decide a case in a particular way. Influencing government officials directly through visits, phone calls, or letters is called *lobbying*. When people want to influence the way Congress handles a law, they lobby their representatives by writing letters or talking to them personally. The lobbying of Supreme Court justices, however, is considered improper because the Court is supposed to make decisions based on the content of the Constitution and not on the political preferences of one or more groups in society.

There is a way, however, for outsiders to submit their views to the Supreme Court. The Court invites interested parties, most often organizations, to submit briefs of *amicus curiae* (*amicus curiae* means "friend of the court"). A party that submits an amicus curiae brief becomes a friend of the Court by giving it information that it may find helpful in making a decision. As the Court explains, "an amicus curiae brief which brings relevant matter to the attention of the Court that has not already been brought to its attention by the parties is of considerable help to the Court. An amicus brief which does not serve this purpose simply burdens the staff and facilities of the Court and its filing is not favored" (*Rules of the Supreme Court* 1990, 45).

In the summer of 1971 the Supreme Court began its review of *Roe v. Wade.* Roe, who was arrested for violating a Texas law forbidding abortions except to save the mother's life, argued that the Texas law was a governmental violation of the right to privacy guaranteed to her by the Constitution. Many national organizations filed amicus curiae briefs in this case. Acting as attorneys on behalf of the National Legal Program on Health Problems of the Poor, the National Welfare Rights Organization, and the American Public Health Association, Alan F. Charles and Susan Grossman Alexander filed a brief of amici curiae (*amici* is the plural of *amicus*) in support of the right to an abortion. The Summary of Argument that Charles and Alexander included in that brief appears below as an example to assist you in writing your own amicus curiae brief:

Brief of Amici Curiae

Summary of Argument

A woman who seeks an abortion is asserting certain fundamental rights which are protected by the Constitution. Among these are rights to marital and family privacy, to individual and sexual privacy; in sum, the right to choose whether to bear children or not. These rights are abridged by the state's restriction of abortions to saving the mother's life. To justify such an abridgment, the state must demonstrate a compelling interest; no such compelling interest exists to save the Texas abortion law.

The state's interest in protecting the woman's health no longer supports restrictions on abortion. Medical science now performs abortions more safely than it brings a woman through pregnancy and childbirth. Any state interest in discouraging non-marital sexual relationships must be served by laws penalizing these relationships, and not by an indirect, overly broad prohibition on abortion. There is no evidence, in any case, that abortion laws deter such relationships. The state's purported interest in expanding the population lacks any viability today; government policy in every other area is now squarely against it. And any purported interest in permitting all embryos to develop and be born is not supported anywhere in the Constitution or any other body of law.

Because of its restriction, the Texas statute denies to poor and non-white women equal access to legal abortions. It is an undeniable fact that abortion in Texas and in virtually every other state in the United States is far more readily available to the white, paying patient than to the poor and non-white. Studies by physicians, sociologists, public health experts, and lawyers all reach this same conclusion. The reasons for it are not purely economic, i.e., that because abortion is an expensive commodity to obtain on the medical marketplace, it is therefore to be expected that the rich will have greater access to it. It is also because in the facilities which provide health care to the poor, abortion is simply not made available to the poor and non-white on the same conditions as it is to paying patients. As a result, the poor resort to criminal abortion, with its high toll of infection and death, in vastly disproportionate numbers.

Largely to blame are restrictive abortion laws, such as the Texas statute, in which the legislature has made lay judgments about what conditions must exist before abortions can be legally performed, and has delegated the authority to make such decisions to physicians and committees of physicians with the threat of felony punishment if they err on the side of granting an abortion. Unlike more privileged women, poor and non-white women are unable to shop for physicians and hospitals sympathetic to their applications, cannot afford the necessary consultations to establish that their conditions qualify them for treatment, and must largely depend upon public hospitals and physicians with whom they have no personal relationship, and who operate under the government's eye, for the relief they seek. The resulting discrimination is easily demonstrated.

Restricting abortion only to treatment necessary to save the mother's life irrationally excludes those classes of women for whom abortion is necessary for the protection of health, or because they will bear a deformed fetus, or who are pregnant due to sexual assault, or who are financially, socially or emotionally incapable of raising a child or whose families would be seriously disrupted by the birth of another child, and these exclusions bear most heavily on the poor and non-white.

In the absence of any compelling state interest, the harsh discriminatory effect on the poor and the non-white resulting from the operation of the Texas abortion law denies to poor and non-white women the equal protection of the laws in violation of the Equal Protection Clause of the Fourteenth Amendment. (Charles 1971, 5–7)

Scope and Purpose

Your task in this chapter is to write an amicus curiae brief for a case that is being considered by the United States Supreme Court. You will write your own brief, making your own argument about how the case should be decided. Of course, you do not have to be entirely original. You will examine the arguments used in others' briefs, add new arguments of your own, and write the entire brief in your own carefully chosen words. In completing this assignment you will also be meeting five more personal learning objectives:

1. You will become familiar with the source, form, and content of legal documents.
2. You will become acquainted with the procedures of brief preparation.
3. You will become familiar with the details of a selected case currently before the Court. As you follow the news reports on this case, you will eventually learn the Court's decision.

4. You will come to understand a Supreme Court case in sufficient depth to be able to integrate the arguments of actual amicus curiae briefs into your own argument.

5. You will learn how to write a clear, logical, effective, persuasive argument.

Remember that your goal is to *persuade* the Supreme Court to make a certain decision. Before you begin, reread the first part of this manual, especially the sections on how to write clearly and persuasively.

General Considerations and Format

Briefs provide the Supreme Court with the facts in a particular case and make arguments about how the case should be decided. The *Rules* of the Court state that "a brief must be compact, logically arranged with proper headings, concise, and free from burdensome, irrelevant, immaterial and scandalous matter. A brief not complying with this paragraph may be disregarded and stricken by the Court" (1990, 28). The Court also requires those who submit an amicus curiae brief to provide a statement of permission, which may be either: (1) evidence that permission to submit the amicus curiae brief has been granted by both parties to the dispute; or if the permission of both parties has not been granted, (2) the reason for the denial and the reason that the Court should consider the amicus brief in spite of the absence of permission of the parties.

Of course, as a student writing an amicus brief for a class in political science, you will not actually submit your brief to the Supreme Court, so you will not need to write a statement of permission. Information on such statements is provided here so that you will understand their purpose when you encounter them in your research.

Ask your instructor about the page limit for your assignment. The Supreme Court's limit for the actual text of amicus curiae briefs (exclusive of the questions-presented page, subject index, table of authorities, and appendix) is thirty pages, single-spaced. Your brief, however, will be double-spaced for the convenience of your instructor and as few as fifteen pages, depending on your instructor's requirements. Because a central purpose of this assignment is for you to understand the arguments to be made in the case, your brief will be shorter than actual amicus briefs submitted to the Court, which require much more detail than you will need to know. As you read actual amicus briefs, use your own judgment to select the material that you believe is most important for the Court to understand, and include this information, in your own words, in your brief.

The proper presentation of briefs is essential. Briefs to the Supreme Court are normally professionally printed, and the *Rules* of the Court include directions for this process. The Court does, however, also accept typed briefs, and your amicus curiae brief will conform to the Court's instructions for typed briefs in most respects, with modifications to allow your instructor sufficient space to write comments. You must therefore prepare your amicus curiae brief according to the following specifications:

- Black type on white paper, $8\frac{1}{2}$ by 11 inches, double-spaced, printed on one side only

- Text and footnotes in 12-point type
- A typeface as close as possible to that used in actual briefs
- Margins of $1\frac{1}{2}$ inches on the left and 1 inch on all other sides
- A binding that meets your instructor's requirements

You will submit one copy of your brief to your instructor. It is always wise, when submitting any paper, to retain a copy for yourself in case the original is lost. (The Supreme Court requires that sixty copies of a brief be submitted for a case coming to it directly under its original jurisdiction, and forty copies for a case coming to it under appellate jurisdiction from lower courts.)

13.2 RESOURCES FOR WRITING AN AMICUS CURIAE BRIEF

You will find resources for amicus curiae briefs in the library and on the Internet. When you conduct your research in the library, you will need access to two periodicals that may be found in some college and in most if not all law school libraries:

- *Preview of United States Supreme Court Cases,* a publication of the American Bar Association's Public Education Division
- *The United States Law Week,* published by The Bureau of National Affairs, Inc. If they are not available in your college library, you may request copies through interlibrary loan, or ask your instructor to request that the department or library order them.

Internet Resources for Writing an Amicus Curiae Brief

Chapter 7 of this manual provides an introduction to political science resources on the Internet. If you are not familiar with the Internet or with political science resources on the Internet, you may want to read the directions in Chapter 7 before proceeding. The Internet provides a wealth of material related to constitutional and international law.

To find cases on the Internet that are currently befor the Supreme Court, go to Cornell University's Legal Information Institute (LLI) (http://supct.law.cornell.edu/supct/). On this page you will find a link entitled "Cases Argued This Term." Peruse the links for current cases, selecting the one that most interests you.

Steps in Writing an Amicus Curiae Brief

Select a Case and a Side

Using the most recent issues of *Preview of United States Supreme Court Cases, The United States Law Week,* or the appropriate Internet sites, select a case and decide which side of the argument you support. The case you choose must fulfill the following two requirements:

1. It must be of personal interest to you.
2. It must be a case that has not yet been decided by the Court.

Obtain Copies of the Amicus Briefs

Your next step is to obtain copies of the briefs on the merits of the appellant and the respondent as well as any available amicus briefs on the side of the case that you support and one amicus brief on the opposing side. There are three ways to obtain amicus briefs. You may obtain them by going in person to the Office of the Clerk of the Supreme Court of the United States at the following address, where you will be allowed to photocopy the briefs (the clerk will not send copies of the briefs in the mail):

> Office of the Clerk
> Supreme Court of the United States
> 1 First Street, NE
> Washington, DC 20543
> Telephone: (202) 479-3000

The second way to obtain the briefs is to request them from the attorneys of record for the organizations that are filing the briefs; *Preview of United States Supreme Court Cases* lists their names, addresses, and telephone numbers. *The United States Law Week* provides this information for some cases and not for others. If this information is not given in either of these publications, you may request it by mail or telephone from the Clerk of the Supreme Court at the above address. Be sure to provide the name and the docket number of the case in which you are interested.

When you contact the attorneys of record, tell them:

> Your name and address
> The college or university you attend
> The nature of your assignment
> The name and docket number of the case in which you are interested
> Your interest in obtaining a copy of their amicus brief
> Your appreciation of their assistance

The third way to obtain the briefs, when they are available, is to print or download them from the appropriate sources on the Internet.

Write an Argument Outline

Read the arguments in the briefs you have collected, and then construct an outline of an argument that makes the points you believe are most important. Your outline should normally have from two to six main points. Follow the directions for constructing outlines that you find in Chapter 1 of this manual, and read Chapter 5 very carefully. Submit your outline to your instructor for advice before continuing.

Write the Argument

Following the outline you have constructed, write your argument. Your writing needs to be clear and sharply focused. Follow the directions for writing in the first part of this manual. The first sentence of each paragraph should state its main point.

The *Rules* of the Court state that the argument of a brief must exhibit "clearly the points of fact and of law being presented and [cite] the authorities and statutes relied upon"; it should also be "as short as possible" (1990, 27). In addition to conforming to page limitations set by your instructor, the length of your argument should be guided by two considerations. First, content must be of adequate length to help the Court make a good decision. All the arguments necessary to making a decision must be present. Write this paper as if you were an officer of the Court. Under no circumstances should you make a false or misleading statement. Be persuasive, but be truthful. You do not need to make the opponents' argument for them, but the facts that you present must be accurate to the best of your knowledge.

The second guideline for determining the length of your argument is to omit extraneous material. Include only the information that will be helpful to the Court in making the decision at hand.

The *Rules* of the Court require that an amicus brief include a "conclusion, specifying with particularity the relief which the party seeks" (1990, 27). Read the conclusions of the briefs you collect, and then write your own, retaining the same format but combining the arguments for the groups you are representing, and limiting your conclusion to two pages.

Write the Summary of Argument

After you have written the argument itself, write the summary, which should be a clearly written series of paragraphs that include all the main points. It should be brief (not more than three double-spaced typed pages). The Summary of Argument written for *Roe v. Wade* that is included at the beginning of this chapter provides an example.

According to the *Rules* of the Court, briefs should contain a "summary of the argument, suitably paragraphed, which should be a succinct, but accurate and clear, condensation of the argument actually made in the body of the brief. A mere repetition of the headings under which the argument is arranged is not sufficient" (1990, 27).

The summary of your argument may be easily assembled by taking the topic sentences from each paragraph and forming them into new paragraphs. The topic sentences contain more information than your subject headings. As complete sentences arranged in logical order, they provide an excellent synopsis of the contents of your brief. Your argument summary should not exceed two pages, double-spaced.

◆ CHAPTER 14 ◆
Public Opinion Survey Papers

14.1 THE SCOPE AND PURPOSE OF A PUBLIC OPINION SURVEY PAPER

A *poll*, most simply, is a device for counting preferences. When we go to the polls on election day, the polling officials count the preferences for candidates (and sometimes laws or other issues) that are produced when people mark their ballots. The officers then transmit these results to local, state, or national officials. A *survey* is a series of statements or questions that define a set of preferences to be polled. If a poll is conducted on the subject of national welfare programs, for example, a survey will be constructed consisting of a series of questions, such as "Do you think that welfare benefits ought to be increased or reduced?" or "Do you believe there is a lot of fraud in the welfare system?"

Writing your own public opinion survey paper will serve two purposes. First, you will learn how to construct, conduct, and interpret a public opinion poll, the means by which much research is done within the discipline. You will thus begin to learn a skill that you may actually use in your professional life. Large and small public and private organizations often conduct polls on the public's needs and preferences in order to make their services more effective and desirable. Second, by writing a survey paper you will understand how to evaluate polls thoughtfully and critically by knowing the strengths and weaknesses of the polling process.

In this chapter you will learn how to construct and conduct a simple public opinion poll and how to apply some elementary data analysis and evaluation techniques to your poll results. Your instructor may want to add supplemental tasks, such as other statistical procedures, and your text in political science methods will tell you much more about the process of public opinion research. The following set of directions, however, will provide the information you will need to create and interpret a public opinion poll.

14.2   STEPS IN WRITING A PUBLIC OPINION SURVEY PAPER

Focus on a Specific Topic

The first step in writing a public opinion survey paper is to select a topic that is focused on one specific issue. Although nationally conducted polls sometimes cover a broad variety of topics, confining your inquiry to one narrowly defined issue will allow you to gain an appreciation for even a single topic's complexity and the difficulties inherent in clearly identifying opinions. Precision is important in clearly understanding public opinion.

Public opinion surveys are conducted on topics pertaining to local, state, national, or international politics, topics nearly as numerous as the titles of articles in a daily newspaper. You will usually increase the interest of the audience of your paper if you select an issue that is currently widely discussed in the news.

Formulate a Research Question and a Research Hypothesis

Once you have selected a topic, your task is to determine what you want to know about people's opinions concerning that topic. If you choose the environment, for example, you may want to know the extent to which people are concerned about environmental quality. You need to phrase your questions carefully. If you ask simply, "Are you concerned about the quality of the environment?" you will probably receive a positive reply from a substantial majority of your respondents. But what does this actually tell you? Does it reveal the depth and strength of people's concern about the environment? Do you know how the respondents will vote on any particular environmental issue? Do people have different attitudes toward air pollution, water quality, and land use? To find out, you will need to design more specific questions. The following sections of this chapter will help you to do this.

To create these specific questions, however, you will first need to formulate a research question and a research hypothesis. Before continuing, read the section in the Introduction to this manual on formulating and testing research hypotheses.

A research question asks exactly what the researcher wants to know. Research questions posed by national polls include the following:

- What is the president's current approval rating?
- What types of voters are likely to favor free trade agreements?
- What is the social issue about which Americans are most concerned?

Research questions for papers for political science classes, however, should be more specific and confined to a narrowly defined topic. Consider the following:

- Is the population to be surveyed in favor of universal handgun registration legislation?

- To what extent do the people polled believe that their own personal political actions, such as voting or writing to a representative, will actually make a difference in the political process?
- What are the attitudes of the selected population toward legislation that promotes gay rights?

Select a Sample

Surveys of public opinion are usually conducted to find out what large groups of people, such as American voters, members of labor unions, or religious fundamentalists, think about a particular problem. It is normally unnecessary and too costly to obtain the views of everyone in these groups. Most surveys therefore question a small but representative percentage of the group that is being studied. The *elements* of surveys are the individual units being studied. Elements might be interest groups, corporations, or church denominations, but they are most often individual voters. The *population* is the total number of elements covered by the research question. If the research question is "Are voters in Calaveras County in favor of a 1 percent sales tax to pay for highway improvements?" then the population is the voters of Calaveras County. The *sample* is the part of the population that is selected to respond to the survey. A *representative sample* includes numbers of elements in the same proportions as they occur in the general population. In other words, if the population of Calaveras County is 14 percent Hispanic and 52 percent female, a representative sample will also be 14 percent Hispanic and 52 percent female. A *nonrepresentative sample* does not include numbers of elements in the same proportions as they occur in the general population.

All samples are drawn from a *sampling frame,* which is the part of the population being surveyed. To represent the population accurately, a sampling frame should include all types of elements (for example, youth, women, Hispanics) of interest to the research question. If the population is the voters of Calaveras County, a sampling frame might be the parents of children in an elementary school who are registered to vote. *Strata* are groups of similar elements within a population. Strata of the voters of Calaveras County may include voters under 30, women, labor union members, or Hispanics. *Stratified samples* include numbers of respondents in different strata that are not in proportion to the general population. For example, a stratified sample of the population of Calaveras County might purposely include only Hispanic women if the purpose of the survey is to determine the views of this group.

A survey research design of the Calaveras County issue would thus be constructed as follows:

Research question: Are voters in Calaveras County in favor of a 1 percent sales tax to pay for highway improvements?

Research hypothesis: Fifty-five percent of the voters in Calaveras County will favor a 1 percent sales tax to pay for highway improvements.

Elements: Individual registered voters

Population: Registered voters in Calaveras County

Sampling frame: Five hundred registered voters in Calaveras County selected at random from voter registration lists

Sample: Of the five hundred registered voters in Calaveras County selected at random from voter registration lists, those who answer the survey questions when called on the telephone

How large must a sample be in order to represent the population accurately? This question is difficult to answer, but two general principles apply. First, a large sample is more likely, simply by chance, to be more representative of a population than a small sample. Second, the goal is to obtain a sample that includes representatives of all of the strata within the whole population.

You will find it most convenient if you use as your sample the class for which you are writing your survey paper. The disadvantage of this sample selection is that your class may not be representative of the college or university in which your survey is conducted. Even if this is the case, however, you will still be learning the procedures for conducting a survey, which is the primary objective of this exercise.

NOTE. Public opinion surveys ask people for their opinions. The people whose opinions are sought are known as *human subjects* of the research. Most colleges and universities have policies concerning research with human subjects. Sometimes administrative offices known as *institutional review boards* are established to review research proposals in order to ensure that the rights of human subjects are protected. It may be necessary for you to obtain permission from such a board or from your college to conduct your survey. *Be sure to comply with all policies of your university with respect to research with human subjects.*

Construct the Survey Questionnaire

Your research question will be your primary guide for constructing your survey questions. As you begin to write your questions, ask yourself what it is that you really want to know about the topic. Suppose that your research question is "What are the views of political science students regarding the role of the government in regulating abortions?" If you ask, for example, "Are you for abortion?" you may get a negative answer from 70 percent of the respondents. If you then ask, "Are you for making abortion illegal?" you may get a negative answer from 81 percent of your respondents. These answers seem to contradict each other. By asking additional questions you may determine that, whereas a majority of the respondents finds abortion regrettable, only a minority wants to make it illegal. But even this may not be enough information to get a clear picture of people's opinions. The portion of the population that wants to make abortion illegal may be greater or smaller according to the strength of the legal penalty to be applied. In addition, some of the students who want no legal penalty for having an abortion may want strict medical requirements imposed on abortion clinics, while others may not. You will need to design additional specific questions in order to accurately determine respondents' views on these issues.

The number of questions to include in your questionnaire is a matter to be carefully considered. The first general rule, as mentioned earlier, is to ask a sufficient number of questions to find out precisely what it is you want to know. A second principle, however, conflicts with this first rule. This principle, which may not be a problem in your political science class, is that people in general do not like to fill out surveys. Survey information can be very valuable, and pollsters are found on street corners, in airports, and on the telephone. Short surveys with a small number of questions are more likely to be answered completely than long questionnaires. The questionnaire for your paper in survey research methods should normally contain between ten and twenty-five questions.

Surveys consist of two types of questions, closed and open. *Closed questions* restrict the response of the respondent to a specific set of answers. Many types of closed questions are used in public opinion surveys, but they may be grouped into three categories:

- Two-choice questions
- Three-choice questions
- Multiple-choice questions

Two-choice questions may ask for a simple preference between candidates, such as: If the election were held today, for whom would you vote: John Kerry or George W. Bush?

Issue-centered two-choice questions offer respondents a choice of one of two answers, most often "yes" and "no," or "agree" and "disagree," as shown below:

Is a mandatory five-day waiting period for the purchase of a handgun desirable?

    Yes   No

A balanced budget amendment to the Constitution should be passed.

    Agree   Disagree

Two-choice questions ask respondents to choose between two statements, neither of which they may entirely support. To find out how many people are ambivalent on these issues, *three-choice questions* are often asked, giving respondents a third selection, which is most often "undecided," "no opinion," "uncertain," "do not know," "does not apply," or "not sure":

The political party that does the most for Hispanic people is

    ☐ Republican   ☐ Democratic   ☐ Uncertain

Simple multiple-choice questions are sometimes constructed to provide a wider range of choices, such as in the following:

If the Democratic primary election were held today, for whom would you vote:

    ☐ Hillary Clinton   ☐ John Edwards
    ☐ Howard Dean   ☐ John Kerry

Just as often, however, multiple-choice questions are constructed to discriminate more clearly between positions in a range of attitudes. For example,

Likert scale multiple-choice questions are used to distinguish among degrees of agreement on a range of possible views on an issue. A Likert scale question might be stated like this:

"American military expenditures should be reduced by an additional 10 percent to provide funds for domestic programs." Select one of the following responses to this statement:

☐ Strongly agree   ☐ Agree   ☐ Not sure
☐ Disagree   ☐ Strongly disagree

Guttmann scale multiple-choice questions allow discrimination among a range of answers by creating a series of statements with which it is increasingly difficult to agree or disagree. A respondent who selects one item on the scale of questions is also likely to agree with the items higher on the scale. Consider this example:

Select the answer with which you agree most completely:

1. Citizen ownership of military weapons such as rocket launchers should be restricted.
2. Citizen ownership of fully automatic weapons such as machine guns should be restricted.
3. Citizen ownership of semiautomatic weapons should be restricted.
4. Citizen ownership of handguns and concealed weapons should be restricted.
5. Citizen ownership of hunting rifles should be restricted.

Closed questions have the advantage of being easy to quantify. A number value can be assigned to each answer, and totals can be made of answers of different types.

By contrast, *open questions*, or *open-ended questions*, are not easy to quantify. In open questions, respondents are not provided a fixed list of choices but may answer anything they want. The advantage of using open questions is that your survey may discover ideas or attitudes of which you were unaware. Suppose, for example, that you ask the following question and give space for respondents to write their answers:

What should be done about gun control?

You might, for example, get a response like the following:

All firearms should be restricted to law enforcement agencies in populated areas. Special, privately owned depositories should be established for hunters to store their rifles for use in target practice or during hunting season.

Open questions call for a more active and thoughtful response than do closed questions. The fact that more time and effort are required may be a disadvantage, because in general the more time and effort a survey demands, the fewer responses it is likely to get. Despite this disadvantage, open questions are to be preferred to closed questions when you want to expand the range of possible answers in order to find out how much diversity there is among opinions on an issue. For practice working with open questions, you should include at least one in your survey questionnaire.

Perhaps the greatest difficulty with open questions is that of quantifying the results. The researcher must examine each answer and then group the responses according to their content. For example, responses clearly in favor, clearly opposed, and ambivalent to gun control might be differentiated. Open questions are of particular value to researchers who are doing continuing research over time. The responses they obtain help them to create better questions for their next survey.

In addition to the regular open and closed questions on your survey questionnaire, you will want to add *identifiers,* which ask for personal information about the respondents, such as gender, age, political party, religion, income level, or other items that may be relevant to the particular topic of your survey. If you ask questions about gun control, for example, you may want to know if men respond differently than women, if Democrats respond differently than Republicans, or if young people respond differently than older people.

Once you have written the survey questionnaire, you need to conduct the survey. You will need to distribute it to the class or other group of respondents. Be sure to provide on the survey form clear directions for filling out the questionnaire. If the students are to complete the survey in class, read the directions out loud and ask if there are any questions before they begin.

Collect the Data

If your sample is only the size of a small political science class, you will be able to tabulate the answers to the questions directly from the survey form. If you have a larger sample, however, you may want to use data collection forms such as those from the Scantron Corporation. You may be using such forms (on which respondents use a number 2 pencil to mark answers) when you take multiple-choice tests in some of your classes now. The advantage of Scantron forms is that they are processed through computers that tabulate the results and sometimes provide some statistical measurements. If you use Scantron sheets, you will need access to computers that process the results, and you may need someone to program the computer to provide the specific statistical data that you need.

Analyze the Data

Once you have collected the completed survey forms, you will need to analyze the data that they provide. Statistical procedures are helpful here to perform three tasks:

1. Describe the data.
2. Compare components of the data.
3. Evaluate the data.

There are many statistical procedures especially designed to carry out each of these tasks. This chapter provides only a few examples of the methods that may be used in each category. Consult your instructor or a survey research methods textbook to learn about other types of statistical measurement tools.

Statistics designed to describe data may be very simple. We will start our discussion with two example questions, both employing the Likert scale:

QUESTION 1

"American military expenditures should be reduced by an additional 10 percent to provide funds for domestic programs." Select one of the following responses to this statement:

☐ Strongly agree   ☐ Agree   ☐ Not sure
☐ Disagree   ☐ Strongly disagree

QUESTION 2

"Congress should provide the Department of Defense with more funding for research into germ warfare techniques." Select one of the following responses to this statement:

☐ Strongly agree   ☐ Agree   ☐ Not sure
☐ Disagree   ☐ Strongly disagree

Our objective in describing the data is to see how our hypothetical respondent sample of forty-two students, as a group, answered these questions. The first step is to assign a numerical value to each answer, as follows:

ANSWER	POINTS
Strongly agree	1
Agree	2
Not sure	3
Disagree	4
Strongly disagree	5

Our next step is to count our survey totals to see how many respondents in our hypothetical sample marked each answer to each question:

ANSWER	POINTS	Q1 RESPONSES	Q2 RESPONSES
Strongly agree	1	8	13
Agree	2	16	10
Not sure	3	12	1
Disagree	4	4	12
Strongly disagree	5	2	6

We may now calculate the mean (numerical average) of responses by performing the following operations for each question:

1. Multiply the point value by the number of responses to determine the number of value points.
2. Add the total value points for each answer.
3. Divide the total value points by the number of respondents (42 in this case).

To see how this procedure is done, examine the chart below, which analyzes the responses to Question 1. Notice that column 1 contains the answer choices provided to the respondents; column 2 contains the point value assigned to each choice; column 3 contains the number of respondents who selected each answer; and column 4 contains the value points assigned for each answer choice, multiplied by the number of responses.

VALUE POINTS

ANSWER CHOICES	ASSIGNED POINT VALUE	NUMBER OF RESPONSES	POINT VALUE × NUMBER OF RESPONSES
Strongly agree	1	8	8
Agree	2	16	32
Not sure	3	12	36
Disagree	4	4	16
Strongly disagree	5	2	10
Total	42	102	
Mean			2.43

We can see that there are 42 total responses and 102 total value points. Dividing the number of value points (102) by the total number of responses (42), we get a mean of 2.43.

If we conduct the same operation for the responses to Question 2 in our survey, we get the following results:

VALUE POINTS

ANSWER CHOICES	ASSIGNED POINT VALUE	NUMBER OF RESPONSES	POINT VALUE × NUMBER OF RESPONSES
Strongly agree	1	13	13
Agree	2	10	20
Not sure	3	1	3
Disagree	4	12	48
Strongly disagree	5	6	30
Total		42	114
Mean			2.71

We see from the table above that the mean of the responses for Question 2 is 2.71. Comparing the means of the two questions, we find that the mean for Question 1 (2.43) is lower than the mean for Question 2. Because the lowest value (1 point) is assigned to a response of "Strongly agree," and the highest value (5 points) is assigned for a response of "Strongly disagree," we know that a high mean score indicates that the sample surveyed tends to disagree with the statement made in the survey question. It is possible to conclude, therefore, that there is slightly more agreement with the statement in Question 1 than with the statement in Question 2. Comparing the mean values in this fashion allows us to easily compare the amount of agreement and disagreement on different questions among the people surveyed.

Another frequently used statistical measure is the standard deviation, which provides a single number that indicates how dispersed the responses to the question are. It tells you, in other words, the extent to which the answers are grouped together at the middle ("Agree," "Not sure," "Disagree") or are dispersed to the extreme answers ("Strongly agree," "Strongly disagree"). To calculate the standard deviation (S) for Question 1, we will follow these steps:

Step 1: Assign a value to each response and the frequency of each response.
Step 2: Find the mean for the question.
Step 3: Subtract the value from the mean.
Step 4: Square the results of Step 3.
Step 5: Multiply the results of Step 4 by the frequency of each value.
Step 6: Sum the values in Step 5.
Step 7: Divide the values in Step 6 by the number of respondents.
Step 8: Find the square root of the value in Step 7, which is the standard deviation.

Our calculation of the standard deviation of Question 1 therefore looks like this:

STEP 1	STEP 2	STEP 3	STEP 4	STEP 5	STEP 6	STEP 7	STEP 8
VALUE (V) AND FREQUENCY (F)	MEAN	MEAN MINUS VALUE	STEP 3 SQUARED	STEP 4 TIMES THE FREQUENCY	SUM OF VALUES IN STEP 5	STEP 6 DIVIDED BY NO. OF RESPOND-ENTS	SQUARE ROOT OF STEP 7: STANDARD DEVIATION
V = 1, F = 8	2.43	1.43	2.04	16.32			
V = 2, F = 16	2.43	.43	.18	2.88			
V = 3, F = 12	2.43	2.57	.32	3.84			
V = 4, F = 4	2.43	21.57	2.46	9.84			
V = 5, F = 2	2.43	22.57	6.6	13.2			
					46.08	1.10	1.05

The standard deviation of Question 1 is 1.05. To understand its significance, we need to know that public opinion samples usually correspond to what is known as a *normal distribution*. In a normal distribution, 68.26 percent of the responses will fall between (1) the mean minus one standard deviation (2.43 − 1.05, or 1.38, in Question 1); and (2) the mean plus one standard deviation (2.43 + 1.05, or 3.48, in Question 1). In other words, in a normal distribution, about two-thirds of the respondents to Question 1 will express an opinion that is between 1.38 and 3.48 on the scale of assigned point values. Another one-third of the respondents will score less than 1.38 or more than 3.48.

For convenience, we will call the responses "Strongly agree" and "Strongly disagree" *extreme responses,* and we will designate "Agree," "Not sure," and "Disagree" as *moderate responses.* We see that a score of 1.38 is closest to our first extreme, "Strongly agree." A score of 3.48 inclines to "Disagree," but is "Not sure." We may conclude that a substantial portion of the respondents (about one-third) tend to give extreme answers to Question 1. We may also notice that the score 1.38, which indicates strong agreement, is closer to its absolute extreme (1.38 is only .38 away from its absolute extreme of 1.0) than is the score 3.48 (which is 1.52 points from its absolute extreme of 5). This means that the responses are slightly more tightly packed toward the extreme of strong agreement. We may conclude that extreme respondents are more likely to strongly agree than to strongly disagree with the statement in Question 1. We can now see more completely the degree of extremism in the population of respondents. Standard deviations become more helpful as the number of the questions in a survey increases, because they allow us to compare quickly and easily the extent of extremism in answers. You will find other measures of dispersion in addition to the standard deviation in your statistical methods textbooks.

After finding the amount of dispersion in responses to a question, you may want to see if different types of respondents answered the question in different ways; that is, you may want to measure relationships in the data. For example, from examining our political party identifier, we find, among our respondents to Question 1, 15 Democrats, 14 Republicans, and 13 independents. To compare their responses, we need to construct a correlation matrix that groups responses by identifier:

ANSWER	DEMOCRAT RESPONSES	REPUBLICAN RESPONSES	INDEPENDENT RESPONSES	TOTAL (FREQUENCY)
Strongly agree	4	2	2	8
Agree	8	4	4	16
Not sure	3	5	4	12
Disagree	0	2	2	4
Strongly disagree	0	1	1	2

Each number of responses in the matrix is found in a location known as a *response cell.* The numbers in the Total (Frequency) column are known as *response total cells.* From this matrix, it appears that Democrats are more likely to agree with the question 1 statement than are either Republicans or independents. If this is true for the sample population, there is a correlation between party affiliation and opinion on the issue.

14.3 ELEMENTS OF A PUBLIC OPINION SURVEY PAPER

A public opinion survey paper is composed of five essential parts:

1. Title page
2. Abstract
3. Text
4. Reference page
5. Appendixes

Title Page

The title page should follow the format directions in Chapter 3. The title of a public opinion survey paper should provide the reader with two types of information: the subject of the survey and the population being polled. Examples of titles for papers based on in-class surveys are "University of South Carolina Student Opinions on Welfare Reform," "Ohio Wesleyan Student Attitudes about Sexual Harassment," and "The 2006 Gubernatorial Election and the Student Vote."

Abstract

Abstracts for a public opinion survey paper should follow the format directions in Chapter 3. In approximately 100 words, the abstract should summarize the subject, methodology, and results of the survey. An abstract for the example used in this chapter might appear something like this:

A survey of attitudes of college students toward the amount of U.S. military expenditures was undertaken in October 2006 at Western State University. The sample was composed of forty-two students in a political science research methods class. The purpose of the survey was to determine the extent to which students are aware of and concerned about recent defense expenditure reductions, including those directly affecting the Seventh Congressional District, in which the university is located, and to determine student attitudes on related defense questions, such as germ warfare. The results indicate a weak correlation between political party affiliation and attitude toward expenditures, with Democrats favoring reductions more than Republicans.

Text

The text of the paper should include five sections:

1. Introduction
2. Literature review
3. Methodology
4. Results
5. Discussion

Introduction

The introduction should explain the purpose of your paper, define the research question hypothesis, and describe the circumstances under which the research was conducted. Your purpose statement will normally be a paragraph in which you explain your reasons for conducting your research. You may want to say something like the following:

> The purpose of this paper is to define Howard University student attitudes toward federal student aid programs. In particular, this study seeks to understand how students view the criteria for aid eligibility and the efficiency of application procedures. Further, the survey is expected to indicate the amount of knowledge students have about the federal student aid process. The primary reason for conducting this study is that the results will provide a basis for identifying problems in the aid application and disbursement process, and facilitate discussion among administrative officers and students about solutions to problems that are identified.

Next, the introduction should state the research question and the research hypotheses. The research question in the above example might be "Is student knowledge of federal student aid programs related to student attitudes about the effectiveness of the programs?" A hypothesis might be "Student ratings of the effectiveness of federal student aid programs are positively correlated with student knowledge of the programs."

Literature Review

A literature review is written to demonstrate that you are familiar with the professional literature relevant to the survey and to summarize that literature for the reader. Your literature review for a public opinion survey paper should address two types of information: the subject and the methodology of the survey.

The subject of the survey, for example, may be a state's proposed secondary education reforms. In this case, the purpose of the subject section of your literature review would be to briefly inform your readers about (1) the history, content, and political implications of the proposed reforms; and (2) the current status of the proposed reforms. In providing this information you will cite appropriate documents, such as bills submitted to the legislature.

The purpose of the methodology section of your literature review will be to cite the literature that supports the methodology of your study. If you follow the directions in this manual or your course textbook to write your paper, briefly state the procedures and statistical calculations you use in the study and the source of your information (this manual or your text) about them.

Methodology

The methodology section of your paper describes how you conducted your study. It should first briefly describe the format and content of the questionnaire. For example, how many questions were asked? What kinds of questions (open, closed, Likert scale, Guttmann scale) were used, and why were these formats selected? What identifiers were selected? Why? What topics within the subject matter were given emphasis? Why? Here you should also briefly address the statistical procedures used in data analysis. Why were they selected? What information are they intended to provide?

Results

The results section of your paper should list the findings of your study. Here you report the results of your statistical calculations. You may want to construct a table that summarizes the numbers of responses to each question on the questionnaire. Next, using your statistical results, answer your research question; that is, tell your reader if your research question was answered by your results and, if so, what the answers are.

Discussion

In your discussion section, draw out the implications of your findings. What is the meaning of the results of your study? What conclusions can you draw? What questions remain unanswered? At the end of this section, provide the reader with suggestions for further research that are derived from your research findings.

Reference Page

Your reference page and source citations in the text should be completed according to the directions in Chapter 4.

Appendixes

See Chapter 3 for further directions on placing appendixes at the end of your text. Appendixes for a public opinion survey paper should include:

- A copy of the questionnaire used in the study
- Tables of survey data not sufficiently important to be included in the text but helpful for reference
- Summaries of survey data from national polls on the same subject, if such polls are available and discussed in your text

NOTE. Students and instructors should note that the applications of the mean and standard deviation suggested in this chapter are controversial because they are applied to ordinal data. In practice, however, such applications are common.

Glossary of Political Science Terms

Accountability   The concept that an elected official is legally, morally, and politically responsible to the voters for his or her actions

Affirmative action   The correcting of discrimination, usually racial in motivation, through government policy

Amendment   A formal action taken by the legislature to change an existing law or bill

Amicus curiae brief   A "friend of the court" brief, filed by a third party to a lawsuit who is presenting additional information to the court in the hopes of influencing the court's decision

Anarchy   Political chaos; as a political movement, the belief that voluntary cooperation among members of a society is better than any form of organized government, because government generally favors one group over others

Antifederalist   One who opposed ratification of the United States Constitution in 1787

Appeal   The process of asking a higher court to consider a verdict rendered by a lower court

Apportionment   The system under which seats in the legislative houses are apportioned among the states

Appropriation   The act of designating funds in the legislature for particular agencies and programs

Aristocracy   A system of government in which power is held by a small ruling class whose status is determined by such factors as wealth, social position, and military power

Authoritarianism   A belief that absolute power should be placed in the hands of one person or a small group

Authority   The power to make, interpret, and enforce laws

Bandwagon effect   The practice of government officials' attaching themselves to a piece of legislation or a political movement because of its popularity

Bicameral legislature   A legislature that is divided into two houses

Brief   A compilation of facts, arguments, and points of law concerning a specific law case, prepared by an attorney and submitted to the court

Bureaucracy   Any large, complex administrative system, but used most often to refer to government in general

Calendar   The agenda listing the business to be taken up by a legislative body

Capitalism   An economic system in which most of the means of production and distribution are privately owned and operated for profit

Caucus   A closed meeting of party officials for the purpose of selecting candidates for government office

Censure   A method by which a legislative body may discipline one of its members

Census   The counting, every ten years, of the total population of the United States, for such purposes as the apportionment of legislators and the determination of direct taxes

Centralization   The concept of focusing power in a national government instead of in state or local governments

Checks and balances   A method of government power distribution in which each major branch of the government has some control over the actions of the other major branches

Circuit court   A superior court that hears civil and criminal cases, and whose judges serve in courts in several jurisdictions or counties, thus going on the "circuit"

Civil rights   The rights of a citizen that guarantee protection against discriminatory behavior by the government or private owners of public facilities

Civil servants   Government employees who are not in the military

Claims court   A court that hears various kinds of claims brought by citizens against the government

Closed primary   A primary election in which only party members may vote

Cloture (closure)   A rule allowing a three-fifths vote of the Senate to end a filibuster

Coattail effect   The tendency of a candidate or officeholder to draw votes for other candidates of his or her party

Collectivism   An economic system in which the land and the means of production and distribution are owned by the people who operate them

Commerce clause   A clause in article 1, section 8, of the U.S. Constitution, giving Congress the power to regulate trade among the states and with foreign nations

Communism   A collectivist social system in which all land and means of production are theoretically in the hands of the people and are shared equally by all individuals

Concurrent powers   Powers shared by state and national governments, including the power to tax and the power to maintain a system of courts

Confederacy   A political system characterized by a weak national government that assumes only those powers granted it by strong state governments

Conservatives   Citizens who resist major changes in their culture and their society; political conservatives tend to favor less government intervention in the social and economic life of the nation

Constituent   An individual who resides in a government official's electoral district

Constitutionalism   A belief in a system of government limited and controlled by a constitution, or contract, drawn up and agreed to by its citizens

Contract theory   An explanation of the relationship of the government to the governed in terms of contractual obligation by consenting parties

Court of appeals   One of twelve national courts in the United States set up to hear appeals from district courts

Dark horse   A candidate for political office who has little chance of winning

Demagogue   A political leader who obtains popularity through emotional appeals to the prejudices and fears of the voters

Democracy   A system of government in which the people govern either directly or through elected representatives

Deregulation   The process of reducing government regulatory involvement in private business

District court   The most basic federal court, where federal cases generally are first heard

Divine right   The belief that a ruler maintains power through a mandate from a Supreme Being

Due process   The right accorded to American citizens to expect fair and equitable treatment in the processes and procedures of law

Electoral college   Electors who meet in their respective state capitals to elect the president and vice president of the United States

Elite theory   The concept that, in any political system, power is always controlled by a small group of people

Faction   A group of people sharing certain beliefs who seek to act together to affect policy

Fascism   A right-wing totalitarian political system in which complete power is held by a dictator who keeps rigid control of society and promotes a belligerent nationalism

Favorite son   A presidential candidate, usually with no chance of winning the party nomination, whose name is placed in nomination at the national convention by the person's home state, usually either to honor that individual or to allow the state's delegation to delay committing their votes to a viable candidate

Federal   A type of government in which power is shared by state and national governments

Filibuster   The Senate process of interrupting meaningful debate on a bill with prolonged, irrelevant speeches aimed at "talking the bill to death"

Franking privilege   The ability of a member of Congress to substitute his or her facsimile signature for a postage stamp and thereby send mail free of charge

Gag rule   A rule limiting the amount of time that can be spent debating a bill or resolution in the legislature

Gerrymandering   Redesigning the boundaries of a legislative district so that the political party controlling the state legislature can maintain control

Grand jury   A group of twelve to twenty-three citizens selected to hear evidence against persons accused of a serious crime in order to determine whether or not a formal charge should be issued

Grants-in-aid   Funding given to state and local governments for them to achieve goals set by the national government

Habeas corpus   A court order requiring that an individual in custody be presented in court with the cause of his or her detention

Ideology   The combined beliefs and doctrines of a group of people that reveal the value system of their culture

Impeachment   The process by which the lower house of a legislature may accuse a high official, such as the president or a Supreme Court justice, of a crime, after which the official is tried by the upper house

Implied powers   Powers held by the federal government that are not specified in the U.S. Constitution but are implied by other, enumerated powers

Incumbent   A political official currently in office

Independent   A voter not registered as a member of a political party

Indictment   A formal accusation, brought by a grand jury, charging a person with a crime

Individualism   The belief in the importance of the needs and rights of the individual over those of the group

Inherent powers   Powers not specified in the U.S. Constitution that are claimed by the president, especially in foreign relations

Initiative   A process by which individuals or interested groups may draw up proposed legislation and bring it to the attention of the legislature through a petition signed by a certain percentage of registered voters

Interest group   An organization of like-minded individuals seeking to influence the making of government policy, often by sponsoring a political action committee (PAC)

Iron triangle   The interrelationship of government agencies, congressional committees, and political action groups, as they influence policy

Item veto   The power of governors in most states to veto selected items from a bill and to approve others

Laissez-faire   A "hands-off" policy rejecting government involvement in the economic system of the state

Left wing   An outlook favoring liberal political and economic programs aimed at benefiting the masses

Legitimacy   The quality of being accepted as authentic; in politics, the people's acceptance of a form of government

Libel   A written statement aimed at discrediting an individual's reputation. *See also* Slander

Liberals   Citizens who favor changes in the system of government to benefit the common people

Libertarians   Advocates of freedom from government action

Lobbyists   People who seek to influence legislation for the benefit of themselves or their clients—usually interest groups—by applying pressure of various kinds to members of Congress

Logrolling   A process by which two or more legislators agree to support each other's bills, which usually concern public works projects

Majority rule   The concept, common in a democracy, that the majority has the right to govern

Monarchy   A political system in which power is held by a hereditary aristocracy, headed by a king or queen

Naturalization   The process by which an alien becomes an American citizen

Natural law   The concept, popularized by eighteenth-century philosophers, that human conduct is governed by immutable laws that are similar to the laws of the physical universe and can, like physical laws, be discovered

Nepotism   The policy of granting political favors, such as government contracts or jobs, to family members

New Left   A liberal political movement begun in the 1960s, largely due to the civil rights movement and the Vietnam War, that brought about widespread reevaluation of political beliefs

Oligarchy   A political system in which power is held by a small group whose membership is determined by wealth or social position

Open primary   A primary election in which voters need not disclose their party affiliation to cast a ballot

Patronage   The power of government officeholders to dole out jobs, contracts, and other favors in return for political support

Pigeonhole   The action of a congressional committee that, by failing to report a bill out for general consideration, ensures its demise

Platform   The set of principles and goals on which a political party or group bases its appeal to the public

Pluralism   The concept that cultural, ethnic, and political diversity plays a major part in the development of government policy

Plurality   The number of votes by which a candidate wins election if that number does not exceed 50 percent of the total votes cast; a plurality need not be a large number of votes, as long as it is a higher number than that claimed by any other candidate

Pocket veto   A method by which the president may kill a bill simply by failing to sign it within ten days following the end of a legislative session

Police power   The power, reserved to legislatures, to establish order and implement government policy

Political action committees (PACs)   Officially registered fund-raising committees that attempt to influence legislation, usually through campaign contributions to members of Congress

Political correctness   A measure of how closely speech, attitude, or policy conforms to certain affirmative action standards. The term is pejorative when used by conservatives warning of liberal attempts at controlling the public's modes of expression and thought processes

Political machine   A political party organization so well established as to wield considerable power

Political party   An organization of officeholders, political candidates, and workers, all of whom share a particular set of beliefs and work together to gain political power through the electoral process

Poll   A survey undertaken to ascertain the opinions of a section of the public

Poll sample   A selection, usually random, of the larger population of individuals polled

Populism   A political philosophy that aims at representing the needs of the rural and poor populations in America rather than the interests of the upper classes and big business

Pork barrel legislation   A congressional bill passed to benefit one specific congressional district, with the aim of promoting the reelection of representatives from that district

Precedent   A court decision that sets a standard for handling later, similar cases

Primary election   An election, held prior to the general election, in which voters nominate party candidates for office

Quorum   The minimum number of members of a legislative body that must be present to conduct business

Ratification   The process by which state legislatures approve or reject proposed agreements between states and proposed amendments to the U.S. Constitution

Reactionary   One who opposes liberal change, favoring instead a return to policies of the past

Recall   A process by which an elected official can be turned out of office through a popular vote

Recidivism   A tendency for criminal offenders to return to criminal habits

Referendum   Method by which voters in certain states can register their approval or dissatisfaction with a bill proposed in their state legislature

Republic   A government that derives its power from the consent of the people, who control policy by electing government officeholders

Reserved powers   Powers of the U.S. Constitution reserved to the state governments

Right wing   An outlook favoring conservative or reactionary political and economic programs

Separation of powers   A method of stabilizing a government by dividing its power among different branches or levels of government

Short ballot   A ballot listing candidates for only a few offices, as opposed to a long ballot, which lists candidates for a great number of offices

Single-issue group   A lobby group attempting to influence legislation concerning only one cause or issue, such as gun control or funding for education

Single-member district   An electoral district from which voters elect only a single representative

Slander   An oral statement intended to damage an individual's reputation. *See also* Libel

Socialism   A political system establishing public ownership and control of the means of production

Sovereignty   The concept that the state is self-governing and free from external control

Split ticket   A situation in which a voter casts ballots for candidates from different political parties

Spoils system   The practice of rewarding supporters and friends with government jobs

Stalking horse   A candidate whose primary function is to set up a constituency and a campaign base for another candidate, deemed stronger by the party, who will be announced later

Statute   A law passed by Congress or a state legislature

Straight ticket   The practice of voting for all candidates on a ballot solely on the basis of their party affiliation

Theocracy   A political system whose leaders assume that their power to govern comes from a Supreme Being who guides the actions of the government

Third party   A political party different from the two traditional parties and typically formed to protest their ineffectualness

Totalitarianism   A political system characterized by state control of cultural institutions and all forms of industry and means of production

Unicameralism   A legislature with only one house or chamber

Unitary   Referring to a political system in which all power resides in the national government, which in turn delegates limited power to local governments

Veto   The process by which the president may send a bill back to Congress instead of signing it into law

Welfare state   A state in which the government is characterized by governmental redistribution of income

Bibliography

Agassiz, Louis. 1958. *A Scientist of Two Worlds: Louis Agassiz.* Ed. Catherine Owens Pearce. Philadelphia: Lippincott.

Carter, Jimmy. 1982. *Keeping Faith: Memoirs of a President.* Toronto: Bantam Books.

Charles, Alan F. 1971. *Motion for Leave to File Brief Amici Curiae in Support of Appellants and Briefs Amici Curiae. Roe v. Wade.* U.S. 70–18, 5–7.

The Chicago Manual of Style. 1993. 14th ed. Chicago: Univ. of Chicago Press.

Esposito, John L., ed. 1997. *Political Islam: Revolution, Radicalism, or Reform?* Boulder, CO: Lynne Rienner Publishers.

Foucault, Michel. 1995. *Discipline and Punish: The Birth of the Prison.* New York: Vintage Books.

Hartwell, Patrick. 1985. "Grammar, Grammars, and the Teaching of Grammar." *College English* 47:105–127.

Kennan, George F. 1967. *Memoirs.* Boston: Little, Brown.

Kennedy, John F. 1963. "John F. Kennedy's Inaugural Address." In *Documents of American History Since 1898.* Vol. 2 of *Documents of American History.* 7th ed. Ed. Henry Steele Commager, 688–689. New York: Appleton-Century-Crofts.

Lamin, Kathryn. 1995. *10,000 Ideas for Term Papers, Projects, & Speeches.* New York: Macmillan.

Lijphart, Arend. 1997. "Unequal Participation: Democracy's Unresolved Dilemma." *American Political Science Review* 91:1–14.

Lincoln, Abraham. 1946. *Abraham Lincoln: His Speeches and Writings.* Ed. Roy Basler. Cleveland, OH: World.

Lunsford, Andrea, and Robert Connors. 1992. *The St. Martin's Handbook.* 2nd ed. Annotated instructor's ed. New York: St. Martin's.

Madison, James, Alexander Hamilton, and John Jay. 1961. *The Federalist Papers.* New York: New American Library/Mentor.

Marx, Karl, and Friedrich Engels. 1965. "Manifesto of the Communist Party." In *Marx and Engels: Basic Writings on Politics and Philosophy.* Ed. Lewis S. Feuer, 6–29. New York: Anchor.

Morgan, A. 1991. *Research into Student Learning in Distance Education.* Victoria: University of South Australia, Underdale.

Morgenthau, Hans J., and Kenneth W. Thompson. 1985. *Politics among Nations: The Struggle for Power and Peace.* 6th ed. New York: Knopf.

President's Committee on Administrative Management. 1937. *Administrative Management in the Government of the United States, January 8, 1937*. Washington, DC: Government Printing Office.

Rawls, John. 1971. *A Theory of Justice*. Belknap Press.

Roosevelt, Franklin D. 1963. "F. D. Roosevelt's First Inaugural Address." In *Documents of American History Since 1898*. Vol. 2 of *Documents of American History*. 7th ed. Ed. Henry Steele Commager, 239–242. New York: Appleton-Century-Crofts.

Rules of the Supreme Court of the United States. 1990. Washington, DC: Government Printing Office.

Scott, Gregory M. 1998. *Review of Political Islam: Revolution, Radicalism, or Reform?* Ed. John L. Esposito. *Southeastern Political Review* 26(2): 512–514.

Thucydides. 1986. *History of the Peloponnesian War*. Trans. Rex Warner. Harmondsworth: Penguin.

Washington, George. 1991. *Washington's Farewell Address to the People of the United States*. 102d Cong., 1st sess. S. Doc. 3.

Index